Harold Kushner
e Print:

You've Ever Wanted Isn't Enough
d Things Happen to Good People

HOW GO
DO WE
HAVE T

HOW GOOD DO WE HAVE TO BE?

A New Understanding of Guilt and Forgiveness

Harold S. Kushner

G.K. Hall & Co.
Thorndike, Maine

Published in 1997 by arrangement with
Little Brown & Co., Inc.

G.K. Hall Large Print Inspirational Collection.

The text of this Large Print edition is unabridged.
Other aspects of the book may vary from the original edition.

Set in 16 pt. Plantin by Juanita Macdonald.

Printed in the United States on permanent paper.

Library of Congress Cataloging in Publication Data

Kushner, Harold S.
    How good do we have to be? : a new understanding of
guilt and forgiveness / Harold S. Kushner.
        p.   cm.
    ISBN 0-7838-2042-9 (lg. print : hc)
    ISBN 0-7838-2043-7 (lg. print : sc)
    1. Good and evil.   2. Eden.   3. Bible. O.T. Genesis III
— Criticism, Interpretation, etc.   4. Self-esteem —
Religious aspects.   5. Perfection — Religious aspects.
6. Guilt — Religious aspects.   7. Forgiveness — Religious
aspects.   8. Religious addiction — Controversial literature.
9. Large type books.   I. Title.
[BJ1401.K87   1997]
296.7—dc21
                                                    96-47723

*For Carl David Haber
with whom the human race begins anew*

ACKNOWLEDGMENTS

I have been fortunate in writing this book, as I have in three previous books, to have had James H. Silberman as my editor. Virtually every page of this book has benefited from his judicious insight. I am grateful to my wife, Suzette, beyond what these words can convey. Her patience with me when I was writing, her support and encouragement when I was pondering what to write next, were invaluable. Several good friends helped me think through what I was trying to say, and I am grateful to them all. Once again, Peter L. Ginsberg, my agent, was matchmaker for this venture, and once again he deserves my profound thanks.

Finally, I must alert the reader to the paradox with which this book begins. This book, whose theme is that we cannot expect people to be perfect, is dedicated to Carl David Haber. Carl Haber is my three-year-old grandson. We think he is perfect.

CONTENTS

INTRODUCTION

I have been thinking about the ideas expressed in this book for a long time. Even as a child, I was bothered by the biblical story of the Garden of Eden. A God who punished people so severely for breaking one arbitrary rule was not a God I wanted to believe in, especially since the story seemed to suggest that Adam and Eve had no knowledge of what good and bad meant before they broke the rule.

As I grew older, I encountered so many instances of people doing what they thought God had done in the Bible, rejecting someone for making one mistake, for not being perfect. When I was rabbi of a congregation in suburban Boston and members of my synagogue would share their problems with me, I would repeatedly hear of children angry at their parents, parents disappointed in their children, husbands and wives upset with each other, brothers not inviting brothers to a wedding because of an argument that had taken place years earlier. The pattern tended to be the same: somebody did something wrong and someone else responded by withdrawing love, sometimes by withdrawing all contact. And the retaliator felt justified in doing that because, after all, hadn't God done the same thing in the Garden of Eden? I often felt frustrated at the inability of my religious perspective to heal that breach.

Fifteen years ago, responding to a personal tragedy, I wrote a book called *When Bad Things Happen to Good People*. Its message was simple but radical: when something bad happens to you, it is not a case of God punishing you because you deserve it. God is on your side, not on the side of the illness or the injury.

This book can be seen as an extension of that earlier one. Its message is equally simple and equally radical: God does not stop loving us every time we do something wrong, and neither should we stop loving ourselves and each other for being less than perfect. If religious teachers tell us otherwise, that is bad religion. If our parents responded to our misbehavior by withdrawing their love, that was a bad response by people who may otherwise have been good parents.

I hope that our sense of self-worth, our relationships to our parents, our children, our mates, our siblings, and friends will improve once we learn the lesson that one mistake need not lead to rejection and banishment. And I hope that this book will guide you to gaining that blessing.

Chapter 1

GOD LOVES YOU ANYWAY

I look out at a synagogue filled to overflowing, every seat taken, people standing in the rear aisle. It is the eve of Yom Kippur, the Day of Atonement, the day on which Jews fast and pray that God forgive their shortcomings and send them forth cleansed to begin the New Year. Men and women who attend no other service during the year come to this one. People who usually arrive halfway through one of our lengthy services make sure to come on time tonight. When the last of the congregants has been seated, I nod to the cantor and he begins to chant the service:

"By consent of the authorities in heaven and on earth, we permit sinners to enter and be part of the congregation."

Who are these sinners whom the opening words of the service admit and welcome? Every one of the nearly one thousand people in attendance believes those words are addressed to him, to her. Religion and conscience have given them the message that they have not always been the people they should have been, and it is to religion that they turn for a message of forgiveness and acceptance.

The liturgy will speak repeatedly of our failings, our neglect of our duties, our hard-heartedness toward others. But if the words of the Day of Atonement are words of rebuke and failure, the "music" carries a very different message. The people in synagogue have not come to be told that they have done things that were wrong. They know that all too well. They have come to be assured that their misdeeds have not separated them from the love of God. They are not looking to be judged and condemned. They are looking to feel cleansed, to gain the confidence and the sense of forgiveness and acceptance that will enable them to begin the New Year without the burden of last year's failures.

There seems to be something in the human soul that causes us to think less of ourselves every time we do something wrong. It may be the result of parents who expected too much of us, or of teachers who took for granted what we did right and fastened instead on everything we got wrong. And maybe it is good for us to feel that way. It may make us more sensitive to what we do wrong and move us to repent and grow. But it may also lead to our setting unrealistically high standards for ourselves and for others.

Religion sets high standards for us and urges us to grow morally in our efforts to meet those standards. Religion tells us, "You could have done better; you can do better." But listen closely to that message. Those are words of encouragement, not condemnation. They are a compliment to our ability to grow, not a criticism of our tendency to make mistakes. We misunderstand the message of religion if we hear it as a message of criticism, even as we misunderstood our parents, thinking they were disappointed in us when what they were trying to do, however awkwardly and maybe unrealistically, was prevent our one day looking back and being disappointed in ourselves for not having done our best. Religion condemns wrongdoing. It takes us to task for lying and hurting people. But religion also tries to wash us clean of disappointment in ourselves, with the liberating message that God finds us worthy of His love.

Dr. Rachel Naomi Remen, a California physician, describes how master psychologist Carl Rogers would approach a therapeutic encounter: " 'There is something I do before I start a session. I let myself know that I am enough. Not perfect. *Perfect wouldn't be enough*. But that I am human, and that is enough. There is nothing this man can say or do or feel that I can't feel in myself. I can be with him. I am enough.' "

Dr. Remen adds, "I was stunned by this. It felt as if some old wound in me, some fear of not being 'good enough,' had come to an end. I knew inside myself that what he said was absolutely true. I am not perfect, but I am enough. Knowing that . . . allows healing to happen."

Not everyone is that wise, to know that they are "good enough" even if they are not perfect. There are a lot of people in the world walking around feeling they are not good enough, feeling disappointed in who they are and not believing they deserve to be loved. We seem to make people feel inadequate wholesale and then try to cheer them up one at a time, but the cure never seems to catch up with the extent of the affliction.

Tolstoy, in the famous opening line of his novel *Anna Karenina*, suggested that "happy families are all alike, but every unhappy family is unhappy in its own way." I am not sure that he was right. My experience as a clergyman and a counselor has taught me that much of the unhappiness people feel burdened by, much of the guilt, much of the sense of having been cheated by life, stems from one of two related causes: either somewhere along the way, somebody — a parent, a teacher, a religious leader — gave them the message that they were not good enough, and they believed it. Or else they came to expect and need more from the people around them — their parents, children, husbands, or wives — than those people could realistically deliver. It is the notion that we were supposed to be perfect, and that we could expect others to be perfect because we needed them to be, that leaves us feeling constantly guilty and perpetually disappointed.

I tend to be suspicious of books and articles that tell us, "Change just one thing in your life and happiness will be yours," whether it is in our eating habits, our work habits, or the way we relate to our husbands and wives. Life is too complicated for a change in one variable to make that much difference. But the more I, as a clergyman, dealt with people's problems and the more I, as a husband, son, father, brother, and friend, learned to look at my own life honestly, the more convinced I became that a lot of misery could be traced to this one mistaken notion: we need to be perfect for people to love us and we forfeit that love if we ever fall short of perfection. There are few emotions more capable of leaving us feeling bad about ourselves than the conviction that we don't deserve to be loved, and few ways more certain to generate that conviction than the idea that every time we do something wrong, we give God and the people closest to us reasons not to love us.

As one who believes in a loving, cleansing, forgiving God and as one who advocates religion as a cure for the afflictions of the soul, I am embarrassed by the use of religion to induce guilt rather than to cure it, and by the number of people I meet, of all faiths, who tell me that they are constantly burdened by feelings of guilt and inadequacy because they "made the mistake of taking religion seriously" when they were children. It is so sad to meet people who think of themselves as deeply religious and to discover that what they think of as religion is in fact a childish fear of losing God's love if they ever do anything against His will.

I would like this book to be a liberating one, because I believe that the essential message of religion is a liberating message, not a restricting or punitive one. I believe that the fundamental message of religion is not

18

that we are sinners because we are not perfect, but that the challenge of being human is so complex that God knows better than to expect perfection from us. Religion comes to wash us clean of our sense of unworthiness and to assure us that when we have tried to be good and have not been as good as we wanted to be, we have not forfeited God's love.

It would be so wonderful to feel good about ourselves again, to be able to rise above the voices of nagging parents, teachers, and other ghosts from our growing-up years and feel we are people to be loved and admired. Religion properly understood can give us that feeling. It is perhaps the best and most valuable thing that religion ever does.

To say that God forgives us for our misdeeds is not a statement about God, about God's emotional generosity. It is a statement about us. To feel forgiven is to feel free to step into the future uncontaminated by the mistakes of the past, encouraged by the knowledge that we can grow and change and need not repeat the same mistakes again.

We may have gotten this message of perfection from parents who genuinely loved

19

us and wanted the best for us, and acted out that concern by correcting our every trivial mistake and constantly urging us to do better. Or we may have gotten it from parents who were emotionally stunted, disappointed in themselves, angry at the world, and incapable of showing us the love and approval we yearned for. And we, in our childish innocence, thought we were responsible for their sour mood and didn't deserve to be loved.

In John Steinbeck's splendid novel *East of Eden*, there is a scene in which a son gives his father a present that he has selected with great care and for which he has sacrificed a great deal. The father spurns it. We, the readers, understand that the father does this because he is an emotionally wounded and constricted person who has trouble seeing his son's better qualities and has trouble believing that he himself deserves a special present. But the boy, lacking the reader's perspective, cannot understand that. The message he gets is that he is not good enough, and that rejection will color the rest of his life.

We may have gotten this message from teachers who praised only perfect papers and showed impatience with us when we got something wrong. We learned that we would have to do perfect work if we ever wanted to hear ourselves praised.

I once observed a second grade class taught by someone with the reputation of being a gifted and creative teacher. She gave a spelling drill by dividing the class into two teams and giving each child on each team a letter of the alphabet. She would then call out a word, and if it included your letter, you had to race up to the front of the room and arrange yourself with your teammates to spell the word out. Your team got points for completing the word first, and lost points for every missing or extra letter. In the course of a half hour, I saw several children sharpen their spelling skills and several other children absorb the lesson that they were slow and stupid and cost their team points. I heard the disappointment and disapproval in the teacher's voice when some children repeatedly made mistakes, and I am sure the children at whom that disapproval was directed heard it too. I left wondering whether on balance it was worth it.

We may have learned to be ashamed of our imperfections from friends and other children who made fun of our physical features, our slowness in the classroom or on the playground. Or saddest of all, we may have learned from our religious leaders, from Bible stories and Sunday School lessons, that God holds us to strict standards of Right and Wrong, that God knows every secret, nasty thing we ever do, even our secret nasty thoughts, and that every sin we commit separates us from God's love. We may have been taught the story of Adam and Eve in the Garden of Eden, how they could have lived happily with God in Paradise but made one mistake and were punished forever for it. And we learned the lesson that if we ever made one mistake, we would lose Paradise and be punished severely.

The starting point of this book is my contention that over the years, Jews and Christians have misunderstood the story of Adam and Eve in the Garden of Eden. We have read it as a story of disobedience and divine punishment, and learned to believe in a God who would punish us severely if we ever did anything wrong. In this book, I will be offering a radically different interpretation of that story, one that will permit us to think better of God and to think better of our first human ancestors as well.

But if we could free ourselves from the notion that God punishes people for doing one thing wrong, if we could come to see God as a God whose love was constant enough to overcome inevitable disappointment, then we would not only like ourselves better, with all the good things that would flow from that. We would be better able to accept our parents' imperfections, their inability to tell us that they loved us and were proud of us, their unrealistic demands and expectations. We would be able to see those things as flaws in them, not criticisms of us, and we would be able to love them despite their flaws even as we believed God loved us despite ours.

Once we stop misunderstanding the Garden of Eden story and learning from it that God expects perfection of us, we could stop expecting perfection from our wives, husbands, and children, asking them to be perfect in order to reflect well on us. We could love them flaws and all, and invite them to love us in the same way. But we won't be able to do that as long as we insist on believing that one mistake is grounds for rejection, whether it is God or we or someone around us who is doing the rejecting.

Elaine Pagels, in a brilliant study of the Christian notion of original sin, *Adam, Eve and the Serpent*, writes, "There is a human tendency to accept personal blame for suffering. *People often would rather feel guilty than helpless.* If the reason for misfortune is moral rather than natural, we can persuade ourselves that we can control it. If guilt is the price to be paid for the illusion of control over nature, many people have seemed willing to pay it." In other words, if we can convince ourselves that we are responsible for sickness, for someone's death, then we can prevent sickness and death by changing our wishes and our behavior.

But the illusion that we can control events if we do everything right, that we can make people love us if we do things right, and that we can guarantee happy endings by deserving them, *is* an illusion, and a very destructive one. No matter how much we love our parents, and no matter how much money we spend on their medical care, they will grow old and die, and we will torture ourselves unnecessarily by thinking we might have prevented it (especially if there is a corner of our brain that remembers a time when we might have wished them harm). No matter how hard we try to be perfect spouses and perfect parents, some marriages will die of natural causes despite our best efforts, and some children will grow up to disappoint us. We just make the situation worse by hitting our heads against the wall and repeating the words "If only I had done something differently."

I don't believe that the story of Adam and Eve is the story of two people who could have lived happily ever after had they done everything right but instead were punished forever for making one mistake. I don't think it means to teach us the lesson that if we ever do something wrong, God will stop loving us and will punish us instead. I don't take the story of the Garden of Eden as a newspaper report of an actual event (though I know that some people do), describing the human race as beginning with two full-grown, Hebrew-speaking adults and a talking snake. But I do believe that the story of the Garden of Eden tells us something profoundly true about the emergence of the human race, and that we will become more comfortable with ourselves as imperfect human beings only when we have learned to understand what the story is really about. If we are to realize the fullness of our humanity, if we are to see our mistakes and even our imperfect successes in an overall context, we can do no better than to begin where the Bible begins, with one man, one woman, one God, and one rule in a brave new world.

Chapter 2

WHAT REALLY HAPPENED IN THE GARDEN OF EDEN?

The story is simultaneously simple and complex, simple enough to tell a child, subtle and profound enough to occupy scholars for a lifetime. It is found in chapter three of the Book of Genesis in the Bible.

In the beginning, God created an orderly, stable world and filled it with plants, birds, and animals. Then, as the crown of His creation, God created a human being in His image, and named him Adam because he had been formed from the earth (in Hebrew, the word for earth is *adama*). He put him in a garden named Eden, and told him to tend it and enjoy its fruits. In the middle of the garden were two special trees, the Tree of Life and the Tree of the Knowledge of Good and Evil. God told Adam that he could eat from any of the plants in the garden, including the Tree of Life, but he was not to eat the fruit of the Tree of the

Knowledge of Good and Evil, "for on the day you eat of it, you will die."

Seeing that Adam was alone and none of the animals was a suitable mate for him, God took one of Adam's ribs (or maybe it wasn't a rib; I'll explain that later) and fashioned a woman, a creature formed of the same human substance as Adam, prompting him to say when he saw her, "This one is bone of my bone and flesh of my flesh." The Bible makes a point of telling us that the first man and the first woman were naked but felt no shame.

At this point, the serpent enters the story, described as "more cunning than all the other animals God had made" and apparently living only to cause trouble. He tempts the woman to eat the forbidden fruit, telling her that God is jealous of her and her mate, and wants to keep all knowledge for Himself. When the woman sees how tempting the forbidden fruit is, she takes it and eats of it, and gives some to her husband, who eats of it as well. Immediately, the Bible tells us, "their eyes were opened and they realized that they were naked." So they sew together some fig leaves to cover themselves.

God appears in the garden, and the man and woman try to hide from Him, explaining that they are hiding because they are naked. God says, "Who told you that you were naked? Have you been eating of that tree that I told you not to eat from?" Adam replies, "It wasn't my fault. The woman You gave me, she talked me into it." The woman similarly tries to excuse herself. "It wasn't my fault, the serpent talked me into it."

God punishes the serpent by condemning it to crawl on its belly and lick dust forever. He banishes the man and the woman from the garden and condemns them to a life of pain and hard work. For the man's punishment, "By the sweat of your brow shall you get bread to eat, until you return to the earth from which you were taken." For the woman's punishment, "I will make most severe your pain in childbirth. . . . Your sexual urge will be for your husband, but he shall rule over you."

Adam and his mate leave the Garden of Eden and settle down outside it to the east. Denied access to the Tree of Life, they become sexually intimate for the first time and have children, Cain, Abel, Seth, and many other sons and daughters. At this point, Adam gives his mate a name, Eve, meaning Source of Life.

That's the story. I can't remember how old I was when I heard it for the first time, but I can remember that, when I was still young, I found some aspects of it hard to understand or accept. You may have had a similar reaction when you first heard it as a child, or when you read this summary of it.

Isn't this a harsh punishment for one small mistake — pain and death, banishment from Paradise, for breaking one rule? Is God really that strict?

Why did God create a tree that He didn't want anyone to eat from? Was God setting Adam and Eve up to disobey so that He could punish them?

Was the woman ever told of the prohibition, either by God or by Adam? Why is the story told in such a way as to make it seem that it was all the woman's fault?

What is the significance of the first humans' being unashamed of their nakedness before they ate the forbidden fruit, and feeling shame immediately afterward?

And perhaps most troubling of all, if the forbidden tree was the Tree of the Knowledge of Good and Evil, does that imply that Adam and his mate had no knowledge of good and evil before they ate of it? If so, how could they have been expected to know that it was wrong to disobey God? And why were they punished if they had no sense of good and evil before they ate of it?

Theologians and philosophers have tried to deal with these questions for thousands of years. They have tried, for example, to make a distinction between *intellectual understanding* of good and evil (knowing that certain things are wrong), which Adam and Eve had before they ate, and *experiential knowledge* of good and evil (knowing what it feels like to do wrong), which they acquired only after eating the forbidden fruit. But somehow that sounds like the sort of distinction that philosophers appreciate, not what the biblical story is about.

By the time of the New Testament, St. Paul had refined the idea into a theological dogma that would be known as Original Sin. As descendants of Adam and Eve, we not only inherit their mortality, the fact that people don't live forever; we inherit their propensity to disobey God.

Saint Augustine, the early Christian philosopher, describes how, as a young man, he and some friends stole pears from a neighbor's orchard, not because they were hungry — they ended up throwing them away — but just for the thrill of doing something wrong, much as youngsters from middle-class homes today might be tempted to shoplift. For him, this was proof of the perversity of the human will, the taint of Adam in each of us, the urge to declare that the rules don't apply to you. (Would Adam and Eve have been as tempted by that one fruit among all the fruits of the garden if it had not been forbidden? Or if the snake had not said to them, "If you eat it, you will be like God"?)

Whereas the Hebrew Bible saw sin as a deed, and saw human beings as capable of atoning for their sin through repentance, changed behavior, and the bringing of a sacrifice, for the early Christians sin has become not a deed but a condition, an ineradicable stain on the human soul. We are not merely people who do some good things and some bad things. We are people who, like Adam, have sinned and become sinners, just as a person who murders one person becomes a murderer and cannot excuse himself by pointing to all the people he did not kill. By sinning, as all human beings, descendants of Adam, inevitably do, we fall short of the perfect obedience to which God has summoned us.

In Archibald MacLeish's masterful play *J. B.*, his modern retelling of the story of Job, the good man who suffers, the three friends who come to "comfort Job" are a Marxist, a psychiatrist, and a clergyman. In response to Job's anguished cry, "What did I ever do to deserve this?" each has his answer. The clergyman tells him:

"Your sin is simple.
  You were born a man . . .
What is your fault? Man's heart is evil.
What have you done? Man's will is evil."

Job replies, "Yours is the cruelest comfort of them all, making the Creator of the Universe the miscreator of mankind." In other words, you are telling me that God made me sinful and is now punishing me for that. God made me flawed and is holding me responsible for being imperfect.

I would like to suggest another way of reading the story, one that I think makes better sense of the events, leaves fewer loose ends, and paints a more positive picture of our first ancestors and by implication of us as well. We don't have to feel condemned by the story, inevitably fated to sin and lose God's love as Adam and Eve did. We can read it as an inspiring, even liberating story, a story of what a wonderful, complicated, painful, and rewarding thing it is to be a human being. I would like to suggest that the story of the Garden of Eden is a tale, not of Paradise Lost but of Paradise Outgrown, not of Original Sin but of the Birth of Conscience.

The account of Adam and Eve eating the fruit of the Tree of the Knowledge of Good and Evil, as I see it, is a mythical description of how the first human beings left the world of animal existence behind and entered the problematic world of being human. It is the biblical account of evolution, seeing the difference between humans and animals in moral rather than in anthropological terms.

For animals, life may be difficult but it is also simple. Food may be hard to come by, they may have to be constantly on guard against predators, but animals never have to make moral decisions. When it comes to killing for food, when it comes to mating, when it comes to protecting their young or sending them off on their own, animals are driven by instinct. Human beings, on the other hand, having eaten of the Tree of the Knowledge of Good and Evil, find issues of supporting their families much more complicated. God's decree that Adam's descendants would earn their bread by the sweat of their brow seems to refer not only to physical labor but to the anxiety that seems to be an inevitable part of a person's earning a living. Unlike the animals, a human being has to choose a career from among the hundreds of possibilities. That person then has to decide how hard to work at that career, balancing it against family obligations, and how honest to be at work. Do you shade the truth to close a sale? Will reducing quality increase profits or just chase away customers? No animal has to worry about those concerns.

Human life is infinitely more complicated than animal life because we are alert to the moral dimensions of the choices we make, and the more authentically human we are, the more complicated our lives become. Could it be that, when God told Adam not to eat the fruit of the forbidden tree, He gave not just a prohibition but a *warning*, like the person telling a friend in line for a promotion, "You know, if you get that job, you'll have more responsibility, less time with your family. You'll have to make decisions that will hurt innocent people. Are you sure you want it?" Might it even be that God *wanted* Adam and Eve to eat the fruit, though He knew it would make their lives painful and complicated and He winced at the pain they would be condemning themselves to, because God didn't want to be the only One in the world who knew the difference between Good and Evil?

Animals can feel pain, but human beings,

because we have eaten of the Tree of Knowledge, can feel a dimension of pain that animals cannot. We can feel loss, dread, frustration, jealousy, betrayal, at levels animals will never know. It is part of the price we pay for our humanity, for our being able to feel love, joy, hope, achievement, faithfulness, and creativity.

One theologian has pointed out that the unusual Hebrew word for pain used in Genesis 3:16–17 when God decrees Adam's and Eve's fate is also used in Genesis 6:6 to describe the pain *God* feels at seeing how badly His world has turned out. Could it be that when God tells Adam and Eve that sexuality, parenthood, and creativity will be painful, He is not so much punishing them as saying to them, "You ate of that tree because you wanted to be like God, knowing Good and Evil? Well, you're about to find out how frustrating it is to be like God, to create something and then give up control of what you have created, to want something to turn out as perfectly as you pictured it in your mind and then see how far short the reality falls of your original intention. There is more pain than you could ever imagine in knowing about Good and Evil."

I see Eve as being terribly brave as she

eats the fruit. She is not frivolous, disobedient, or easily seduced, as later interpreters have insisted on describing her. She is boldly crossing the boundary into the unknown, venturing to discover what lies beyond the limits of animal existence, and reaching back to bring Adam after her. The portrait of Eve in Genesis calls to mind the Greek myth of Pandora (described in some versions of the story as the first woman on earth). Pandora was given a box and told never to open it. Inevitably she did, and all manner of troubles and diseases flew out to plague the world ever after. One suspects that the original story has been distorted, as the Garden of Eden story has been misinterpreted, to paint the woman as the villain responsible for all the world's problems. The name Pandora means "all gifts" in Greek, and one might speculate that in the original story, the box contained all sorts of *good* things the gods wanted to keep from mankind. In the same way, I read the story of the garden not as an account of Eve imposing Sin and Death on her descendants, but as an account of her giving us humanity, with all of its pain and all of its richness. Like Pandora, the donor of "all gifts," Eve has given her descendants more than existence; she has given us Life.

When Adam and Eve outgrow the world of animal existence and enter the complicated world of human moral expectations, they become uncomfortable at being judged and scrutinized. They realize that the choices they have to make are so immensely complicated that they can't possibly always get them right. They will inevitably make mistakes. In that sense, they are like adolescents. Have you ever noticed that ten- and eleven-year-old boys and girls are almost always serenely confident about themselves and the things they do? Think of the comic strips and situation comedies in which the youngest child is good at school, runs a lemonade stand, and plays computer games, while his older sister is constantly mooning over boys and waiting for the phone to ring. When youngsters reach adolescence and begin to take responsibility for difficult moral choices (they have tasted the fruit of the Knowledge of Good and Evil, moral and sexual), they become exquisitely self-conscious, convinced that everyone is watching and evaluating them, their looks, their clothes, their complexions. The eleven-year-old who called, "Momma, come see what I can do," becomes the sullen four-teen-year-old who says, "Ma, will you get off my case and leave me alone."

Adam and Eve, brand-new in the world of knowing Good and Evil, are like that. They try to hide from God; if they can't be found, if they can't be seen, they can't be judged. God summons them and they have to respond. Rather than claiming they could not have been expected to know better, they acknowledge their new status as morally aware human beings by admitting that something wrong happened. But they try to blame other people for not having known better. Adam blames Eve for giving him the fruit, and even blames God for having given him Eve. Eve blames the serpent. Having eaten the fruit and learned to speak the language of Right and Wrong, they now claim that they are blameless and (literally) everyone else in the world is wrong. Our first ancestors try to defend themselves against God's accusations by claiming, "I'm not guilty. It wasn't my fault; someone else made me do it." They are saying, in effect, "Yes, there is such a thing as responsibility, but we're not responsible."

Unimpressed by their excuses, God decrees that henceforth Adam will have to work for his food, earning his bread by the sweat of his brow instead of searching for it as animals do. Eve will find childbirth and child-rearing painful. And both of them will live in dread of the day they will die and return to the dust from which they were first fashioned.

At first glance, those edicts sound like punishments, and they have been understood that way for most of history. Adam ate the forbidden fruit, so now he will have to till the soil to make food grow instead of being able to pick it from the trees. Eve gave in to appetite, so her sexual appetite will cause her no end of pain and problems. They spurned the Tree of Life to eat of the Tree of Knowledge instead, so they will not live forever but will die, and will know that they will.

But look at those verses with fresh eyes, without the presumption that this is a story of misbehavior and punishment. Work, sexual intimacy, parenthood, a sense of mortality, the knowledge of good and evil — aren't those precisely the things that separate us from the animal kingdom? Those are the sources of creativity, the things that make us human. They may be painful, but it is the sort of pain that leads to growth, like the burden of being a decision-making executive rather than a factory worker or the problems of being an involved parent rather than remaining childless.

Animals mate to reproduce. Some animals

mate for life, seem to find companionship in each other, and grieve when their mates die. But animals couple sexually only to reproduce, only to satisfy a powerful instinct. We have no reason to believe that animals other than human beings ever come together sexually for reasons of intimacy, pleasure, or love. As far as we know, with very rare exceptions, animals don't seduce or betray, nor do they withhold sexual favors out of anger or jealousy. The sexual life of animals is much simpler, and much shallower, than that of humans. It holds less danger of pain, whether physical or emotional, and is a less-efficient way of reproducing the species.

It has been pointed out that human beings are the only living creatures that make love face to face, because only with human beings does it matter who your partner is. It has been noted that human beings are unique in being capable of sexual arousal even when they are not in a position to become pregnant, because for humans, and for humans only, sex is about love and intimacy and shared pleasure, not only about heeding the instinct to reproduce. That is why, when I was a congregational rabbi, I would not hesitate to officiate at the marriage of a couple who were past childbearing age or were infertile for reasons of illness or surgery.

The pain decreed on Eve, the pain of bearing children, does not end with childbirth. It is infinitely harder to be a human parent than to be an animal parent. I have seen calves born, and I have seen them get to their feet and start walking around within minutes of their birth. Their mothers had to nurse them, but beyond that had few responsibilities. The newborn calves will never have to be taught. They are born "hardwired" with everything they will ever need to know.

But human newborns are a very different story. It is part of the pain and the glory of being human that so little of our behavior is covered by instinct, and so much has to be learned. Unlike the calf, my grandson took nearly a year to learn to walk. He will spend a significant percentage of his life learning the things he needs to know. At some point, there will be an extraordinary moment in his life, one which no other species can ever experience, when he will come to understand that certain things are expected of him, that some things are right and others are wrong. It is not just a matter of being praised or punished; animals can understand that. It is a matter of hearing a voice inside himself that only human beings can hear. Even as dogs can hear high-pitched tones that we cannot, we hear cries of conscience to which animals are deaf. It may come to my grandson when he spontaneously shares a toy with another child, or when someone shares with him. It may happen when he is caught doing something wrong and is forgiven, and taught that parental love is constant and dependable, not to be withdrawn every time he goes astray. Some of that educational process may well be ineffective, and some may be difficult. But the result, one hopes, will be that rarest and most wondrous of creatures, an authentic human being.

As Eve's descendants cannot look forward to problem-free childbirth and child-rearing, Adam's descendants will not only have to share in the parenting (as some, but not all, males do in the animal kingdom). They (and in all likelihood, their wives) will have to work. For human beings, there is an extra dimension, a uniquely human dimension, to work as there is to sex. Shakespeare wrote his plays, and Mozart his symphonies, to earn money to feed their families, but they also did it to be creative, to make use of their talents, to leave something of themselves behind when their lives ended. Perhaps because they knew they would one day die, they were driven to leave something of themselves behind. It has been said that a person should do three things in his or her life: have a child, plant a tree, and write a book. That is, we strive to defeat death by investing ourselves in things that will outlast us. Men name their companies after themselves. They spend hours working for charitable causes. Women, many of them with demanding professional responsibilities, chair church and synagogue committees, raise money for medical research, and volunteer for the League of Women Voters. It is often hard and frustrating work, but they do it so that their communities can be better places to live. Only a human being, whose ancestors ate of the Tree of the Knowledge of Good and Evil, can understand why we do that.

I am suggesting that the story of the Garden of Eden is not an account of people being punished for having made one mistake, losing Paradise because they were not perfect. It is the story of the first human beings graduating, evolving from the relatively uncomplicated world of animal life to the immensely complicated world of being human and knowing that there is more to life than eating and mating, that there are such things as Good and Evil. They enter a world where they will inevitably make many mistakes, not because they are weak or bad but because the choices they confront will be such difficult ones. But the satisfactions will be equally great. While animals can only be useful and obedient, human beings can be good. The story of the Garden of Eden is not a story of the Fall of Man, but of the Emergence of Humankind.

I don't believe that eating from the Tree of Knowledge was sinful. I believe it was one of the bravest and most liberating events in the history of the human race. Yes, its consequences were painful, in the same way that growing up and leaving your parental home can be painful, in the same way that undertaking the responsibilities of marriage and parenthood can be painful and leave you wondering, "Why did I ever give up my less-complicated life for these problems?" But for the person who has experienced the complex, hard-earned satisfactions of human existence, there is no doubt that it is worth the pain.

The woman is not the villain of the story, enslaved by appetite and bringing sin and death into the world. She can be seen as the heroine of the story, leading her husband into the brave new world of moral demands and moral decisions.

And religion is not the carping voice of condemnation, telling us that the normal is sinful and the well-intentioned mistake is an unforgivable transgression that will damn us forever. Religion is the voice that says, I will guide you through this minefield of difficult moral choices, sharing with you the insights and experiences of the greatest souls of the past, and I will offer you comfort and forgiveness when you are troubled by the painful choices you made.

To say that human beings do wrong things, to say that they are capable of cruelty and deceit far worse than any other creature, to say that nobody will ever lead a perfect life any more than any baseball player will ever bat 1.000, is a statement about human beings and the complexity of the choices we have to make. To say that we are destined to lose God's love or to go to Hell because of our sins is not a statement about us but about God, about the tentative nature of God's love and the conditional nature of God's forgiveness. It is a claim that God expects perfection from us and will settle for nothing less. I agree with the first concept, the fallibility of human beings. I strenuously reject the second. If I am capable of forgiveness, of recognizing intermittent weakness in good people or good intentions gone astray in myself and in others, how can God not be capable of at least as much?

HOW THE STORY MIGHT HAVE ENDED

So the woman saw that the tree was good to eat and a delight to the eye, and the serpent said to her, "Eat of it, for when you eat of it, you will be as wise as God." But the woman said, "No, God has commanded us not to eat of it, and I will not disobey God."

And God called to the man and the woman and said to them, "Because you have hearkened to My word and not disobeyed My command, I shall reward you greatly." To the man, He said, "You will never have to work again. Spend all your days in idle contentment, with food growing all around you." To the woman, He said, "You will bear children without pain and you will raise them without pain. They will need nothing from you. Children will not cry when their parents die, and parents will not cry when their children die." To both of them, He said, "For the rest of your lives, you will have full bellies and con-

tented smiles. You will never cry and you will never laugh. You will never long for something you don't have, and you will never receive something you always wanted." And the man and the woman grew old together in the garden, eating daily from the Tree of Life and having many children. And the grass grew high around the Tree of the Knowledge of Good and Evil until it disappeared from view, for there was no one to tend it.

Chapter 3

I THOUGHT I HAD TO BE PERFECT

The first thing that happens to Adam and Eve when they enter the world of knowing good and evil is that they feel shame at the experience of having their misbehavior exposed. Their nakedness is a symbol, a physical manifestation of their being seen when they would rather not be seen. (Freud theorized that the nearly universal dream of finding ourselves in public only partially dressed is a symbolic expression of our fear that if people examined us closely, they would judge us inadequate.) Rather than guilt ("We have done something we should not have done"), they feel shame ("We are being judged as bad people"). Just as adolescents are exquisitely self-conscious, convinced that everyone is looking at them and judging their looks, their clothes, their hair, Adam and Eve, so new to the world of being grown-up humans, have this sense of being exposed and evaluated. In the biblical image, they realize that they are naked and seek to cover themselves. Before they ate from the Tree of Knowledge, the Bible makes a point of telling us, they were as naked as the rest of the animals and like the animals, they felt no shame. But once they rose above the animal level and came to understand that some things are right and others wrong, they gained a sense of self-consciousness, a sense of being held to a standard in a way that no other animal is. It is not that being naked was immoral, rather that a person with a sense of morality knows the feeling of being scrutinized and judged.

When Charles Darwin shocked the nineteenth-century world with his theory that human beings and apes had a common ancestry, someone asked him whether there was still anything unique about the human being. Darwin answered, "Man is the only animal that blushes." That is, human beings are the only creatures capable of recognizing the gap between what they are and what they can be expected to be, and of being embarrassed by that gap.

We tend to use the words *guilt* and *shame* more or less interchangeably, as synonyms for feeling bad about ourselves. But psychologists and anthropologists see them as different emotions. Basically, they see guilt as feeling bad for what you have *done or not done,* while shame is feeling bad for who you *are,* measured against some standard of perfection or acceptability. The distinction is crucial, because we can atone for the things we have done more easily than we can change who we are. But human nature being what it is, we move so easily from one to the other. We hear criticism of something we have done, and translate it into a comment about what sort of person we are. We assume it is our worth as a person, not just our behavior, that is being judged and found wanting. The schoolchild assumes that his report card is evaluating him as a person, not just his spelling and math performance. So a bad grade means "I am bad" and a failing grade means "I am a failure." A youngster overhears his or her parents saying, "She's so shy around other children," "He's so much shorter than other boys his age," and feels a sense of shame for having disappointed the parents.

I read recently that at the finals of the National Spelling Bee, where the best school-age spellers in the country come to compete, the organizers have had to set up a "comfort room" where contestants can go to cry in private and vent their frustrations on a punching bag, to try to cope with the shame and sense of failure that come with having gotten one word wrong after having spelled hundreds of words correctly. I can believe that. To this day, I cannot see the word "judgment" without remembering that nearly fifty years ago, that was the word I got wrong in the opening round of a school-wide spelling bee that I confidently thought I would win (like Vice President Quayle, I put in an extra "e"), and still feel the disappointment over that mistake.

I can remember so many occasions from my growing-up years and my life as an adult, occasions of feeling shame, feeling I had disappointed people who were judging me and fallen short of what I wanted to be — giving wrong answers, forgetting my lines in a play, tripping over myself in a game, coming up with an embarrassing slip of the tongue. What I find remarkable is not that those things happened — it would have been more remarkable if none of those things ever happened — but that years and decades later, after a life rich in achievements and satisfaction, I can still remember them, and the longer I think about it, the more such moments I can still remember, and they still have the power to hurt.

One would expect world-class athletes to demand perfection of themselves in every play, every performance. But studies have shown that the athletes who obsess over their mistakes ("I lifted my head too soon; I forgot to shift my weight forward; I've got to do it right this time") do much worse than athletes who say to themselves, "That wasn't very good; the next one will be better." I can think of outstanding athletes whose careers were ruined because they could not get over having made one mistake at a crucial moment. In 1986, an outstanding major league relief pitcher, Donnie Moore of the California Angels, needed to get one more out to put his team into the World Series. Instead he gave up a home run that ended up costing his team the game and the championship. A few years later, Donnie Moore tragically took his own life, his years of athletic success obliterated in his mind by that one mistake. And I can think of others who overcame that sort of failure. A few years ago, a nineteen-year-old college basketball player, Chris Webber, made a mental mistake in the national championship game, calling a time-out when his team had already used up all of its time-outs and thereby losing possession of the ball in the last seconds of a close game. But Webber refused to let that one play define him, knowing himself well enough to believe that he could be an outstanding player even if not a perfect one. A year later, he was professional basketball's Rookie of the Year.

In the same way, dieters who berate themselves for every lapse ("What's wrong with me? Why did I have that dessert? Why can't I ever stick to a diet?") don't lose as much weight as those who say, "Oh well, a few days of being careful will make up for that." When we let ourselves be defined in our own minds by our worst moments instead of our best ones, we learn to think of ourselves as people who never get it right, rather than as capable people who make an occasional, thoroughly human mistake.

When religion teaches us that one mistake is enough to define us as sinners and put us at risk of losing God's love, as happened to Adam and Eve in the traditional understanding of the story, when religion teaches us that even angry and lustful *thoughts* are sinful, then we all come to think of ourselves as sinners, because by that definition every one of us does something wrong, probably daily. If nothing short of perfection will permit us to stand before God, then none of us will, because none of us is perfect. Under that definition of sin, our lives will be dominated by feelings of guilt and fear, guilt for the mistakes we have made, and fear of making yet another one. And guilt and fear don't bring out the best in anyone. They drain the joy out of life and make us unpleasant companions.

But when religion teaches us that God loves the wounded soul, the chastised soul that has learned something of its own fallibility and its own limitations, when religion teaches us that being human is such a complicated challenge that all of us will make mistakes in the process of learning how to do it right, then we can come to see our mistakes not as emblems of our unworthiness but as experiences we can learn from. We will be brave enough to try something new without being afraid of getting it wrong. Our sense of shame will be the result of our humility, our learning our limits, rather than our wanting to hide from scrutiny because we have done badly.

Psychologists make a second distinction between guilt and shame. Guilt, they say, is a judgment we pass on ourselves. It is a voice inside our heads telling us that we did something wrong. Shame is a sense of being judged by someone else. It is visual rather than auditory, not an inner voice but a sense of being exposed, being looked at and judged by someone whose opinions we take seriously. Shame is what a girl feels when no one asks her to dance, what a young boy experiences when he is the last to be chosen for a team. Guilt is the product of an individual conscience. A psychopath, a person without a conscience, will do terrible things and not feel guilty. Shame is the product of a community. If we don't care about what other people think of us, we will feel no shame.

At one level, there is something positive and vital about feeling guilt and shame. They are an essential part of being human, and while being human is often painful and problematic, when we rise to the challenge, it can be immensely fulfilling. Being judged may make us feel uncomfortable, but being ignored, getting the message that no one cares what we do because nothing we do is that important, can make us feel worse. A colleague of mine says, "The purpose of guilt is to make us feel bad for the right reasons so that we can then feel good for the right reasons." And psychiatrist Willard Gaylin writes, "Shame and guilt are necessary for the development of some of the most elegant qualities of human potential. . . . They are not useless emotions. They signal to us that we have transgressed codes of behavior which we personally want to attain." If Man is the only creature that blushes, then a person who cannot feel shame (like Adam and Eve before they ate from the Tree of Knowledge) is less than completely human.

But carried too far, feelings of shame and guilt stop being beneficial and become harmful. It has been said, "A sensitive conscience is a fine servant but a terrible master." We want to be judged because to be judged is to be taken seriously, and not to be judged is to be ignored. But at the same time, we are afraid of being judged and found flawed, less than perfect, because our minds translate "imperfect" to mean "unacceptable, not worth loving." We make the facile translation from "I have done some wrong things" to "I am a person who constantly does wrong things" to "Anyone who really gets to know me will discover that I am bad and will reject me." Some of us become so preoccupied with insisting that we are perfect, so insistent on lying to protect ourselves and on finding someone to blame, so determined never to lose an argument, that we don't notice how obnoxious we become in the process. We condemn ourselves to the uncomfortable posture of constantly pretending to be someone we really are not, someone flawless and perfect, because we think we have to do that to be lovable. We overreact to the mildest and most innocent of criticisms as if they were attacks on our worth as people. Bestselling author Deborah Tannen recalls how, during an interview, the photographer who was supposed to take her picture realized he did not have the right lens. Instead of admitting that he had forgotten it, he explained, "The lens didn't accompany us." I wonder what terrible thing he thought might have happened had he admitted he made a mistake.

We need to learn that saying, "I'm sorry, I messed that up," inspires more admiration than "Don't blame me; it was someone else's fault." John F. Kennedy, confident in his ability to make people love him, could take responsibility for the failed invasion of Cuba, and the nation admired him for it. Richard Nixon, ever insecure in his ability to inspire affection despite his many achievements, chose to "stonewall" the Watergate investigation and ended up leaving the White House in disgrace.

The question is not whether or not we will make mistakes, whether or not we will get some important things wrong from time to time and feel terrible about it. Of course we will. Anyone who takes the moral demands of a human life seriously will make his or her share of mistakes. The question is, how shall we deal with our imperfection, our sense of inadequacy? How do you relieve guilt? How do you cure shame?

As an advocate of religion as a primary source of spiritual nourishment, I am deeply embarrassed by the tendency of so many religious spokesmen to play on our vulnerability to guilt and shame as a way of controlling our behavior. They teach us that normal sexual acts and thoughts during adolescence (and afterward) are sinful. They warn us that normal emotions like pride and anger are counted among the Seven Deadly Sins. (A therapist friend of mine had as a client a devout Southern Baptist woman who would not permit herself to get angry, no matter how badly she was mistreated, because she believed that anger was a sin. The therapist directed her to read through the Bible and write down all the passages in which God or Jesus gets angry.) They prey upon our feelings of being inadequate caretakers of our parents and inadequate parents to our own children, saying things like, "Why can one mother care for four children, but four children can't care for one mother?"

I have often been amused to hear Protestants, Catholics, and Jews compete over the question of whose religious education was more guilt-producing. The answer is that none of these religions make normal people feel guilty when religion is properly taught and properly understood, when it has realistic expectations of us and introduces us to a loving God, and any one of them makes us feel guilty when religion uses our inevitable human shortcomings to manipulate our emotions and make us feel unworthy. Religion properly understood is the cure for feelings of guilt and shame, not their cause.

The authentic religious question is not the one that may have occurred to Adam and Eve: "Why did we do that when God didn't want us to?" The authentic religious question is: What do we do with our feelings of inadequacy when we have disappointed God? Where do we bring our broken souls to have them mended? How do we armor ourselves against the dreaded feeling of being examined and found wanting?

Yes, religion can make us feel guilty by setting standards for us, holding up ideals against which we can measure ourselves. But that same religion can then welcome us in our imperfection. It can comfort us with the message that God prefers the broken and contrite heart that knows its failures over the complacent and arrogant one that claims never to have erred. Biblical scholars write of the complementary functions of prophet and priest among the Israelite people. The prophet would point out the people's shortcomings and urge them to repent, warning them of God's judgment, saying to them in God's name: "I will love you only if you deserve it, if you change your behavior and earn my love." The priest, by contrast, offered a gentler, more forgiving love: No matter what you have done, you are always acceptable here. (One recalls the poet Robert Frost's line "Home is the place where, when you have to go there, / they have to let you in.") The prophet chastised sinners, the priest welcomed them to the altar. We need both, as ancient Israel needed both. We need the demanding voice of the prophet to hold us to high standards, so that we can grow and be all that we are capable of being. We need to be told that God loves us because we are in fact lovable people, because we deserve love, because we have earned it. And we need the comforting voice of the priest to assure us that even when we don't feel we deserve to be loved, God loves us anyway because He is a loving, forgiving God who knows us too well to expect more from us than we are capable of being.

Several years ago, I was invited to speak

at Johns Hopkins Medical Center in Baltimore, Maryland. I was asked to talk to the professional staff — doctors, nurses, chaplains, social workers — at noon, and then deliver a public lecture in the evening. After my noon talk to the staff, the chief of chaplaincy services came up to me and said, "Rabbi Kushner, we have a patient here at the hospital who would love to meet you. He heard you were going to be here, he has read all of your books and benefited from them, and he just wanted the chance to talk to you. Let me be clear about this. You're certainly under no obligation to see him. If you'd rather not, I'll tell him that you were tired and had a very full schedule. He is a thirty-two-year-old Episcopal minister, and he's dying of AIDS." I indicated that I would be willing to see him. The chaplain led me down a corridor and into a room where I saw a pale, emaciated figure lying in a bed and hooked up to several intravenous tubes. I introduced myself and asked him how he was doing. "Not too good," he told me, "but I'm getting used to it." I asked him, "Do you ever worry that you might be dying without God? That your disease might in some way be a punishment from God for something you did?" He looked up at me and said, "No, just the opposite. The only good thing that has come out of this is that I found out that something I always wanted to believe is really true. No matter how much I may have messed up my life, God hasn't given up on me. I've felt His presence here in this hospital room. He can love me even when I find it hard to love myself."

He paused to gather his strength before continuing. "When I was young, I thought I had to be perfect for people to love me. My parents gave me that message, threatening to withhold love every time I offended them. My teachers at school gave me that message. My Sunday School teachers reinforced that lesson. We didn't go to one of those hellfire-and-brimstone churches, but we heard a lot about how much pain we were causing God every time we sinned, and I think that was just as bad, especially given the list of things we were told were sins.

"I tried so hard to be perfect so that my parents, my teachers, and God would love me. I probably went into the ministry in part so that people would think that I was morally perfect and love me for it. But every time I did something that I knew was wrong, and every time I told a lie to cover up for myself, I would hate myself for being such a phony, and I was sure that God was as contemptuous of me as I was of myself.

"But lying here in this hospital bed, knowing I'm going to die soon, I had this insight: God knows what I'm like and He doesn't hate me, so I don't have to hate myself. God knows what I've done and He loves me anyway. I'll be leaving the hospital soon, not because I'm getting better but because there's nothing more they can do for me and they need the bed for somebody they can help. I don't know if my congregation will take me back, now that they know I'm gay and have AIDS and I'm dying. I hope they will, because there is one last sermon I want to preach to them. I have to share with them the lesson my illness has taught me: You don't have to be perfect. Just do your best, and God will accept you as you are. Don't expect your children to be perfect. Love them for their faults, for their trying and stumbling, even as our Father in Heaven loves us."

At the supermarket checkout counter, I notice five women's magazines offering diet advice on their covers. I see the woman waiting on line ahead of me contemplating those same covers, and I wonder what is going through her mind as she does so. Is she feeling bad because her figure doesn't qualify her to be a fashion model? Has she been brainwashed to feel inadequate as a person for not meeting society's expectations of attractiveness? Or is she wise enough to remember that age and genetics play dirty tricks on all of us? If the woman on line in front of me is divorced, she may feel not that her marriage failed but that *she* failed by not being the perfect sexual partner she should have been, a feeling reinforced by the magazines' tendency to suggest that women are responsible for the emotional health of a relationship. At its worst, she may be driven to anorexia or bulimia, almost exclusively women's afflictions, out of a sense of shame that her body isn't as perfect as the bodies of the models and movie stars held up as prototypes for her.

Psychologists suspect that anorexia, starving oneself to the point of illness and sometimes death, results from a sense of self-loathing, a disgust with one's body. Women hate their bodies, are ashamed of their bodies, because society has taught them that they are evaluated by their appearance. Their looks define who they are. Gather a hundred women at random and ask them how they feel about their looks, their hair, their figures, and I would guess that between ninety-five and one hundred of them would express some dissatisfaction. I have known strikingly attractive women who would become depressed over a five-pound weight gain or a barely visible cosmetic blemish. Entire industries — fashion, cosmetics, perfume, low-calorie foods, bestselling diet books, plastic surgery, weight loss clinics — have been built on the foundation of women's feeling ashamed of their appearance, to the point where one could speculate that if all the women in America were to wake up one morning feeling good about themselves, the American economy would collapse.

And at the heart of all this shame is the notion that to be acceptable, to be lovable, a woman has to measure up to some unrealistic standard of perfection (when all the while, the sad truth is that women who like themselves and are comfortable with who they are are much more pleasant company than women who are constantly depriving themselves and trying to hide their feelings of disappointment in themselves).

Is there a male equivalent of anorexia? What drives men to self-loathing and self-destructive behavior? If society teaches women to feel ashamed of themselves for being too fat or unattractive, it teaches men to feel ashamed for not making a lot of money. (And now that more women are entering the business world, they too are learning to feel disappointed in themselves for not being financially successful.) For every woman's magazine with an article on weight loss, there is a book for men on how to be a better salesman or a more effective manager. And for every actress on television or in the movies with perfect hair and a flawless figure, there is a male companion with a well-tailored suit and driving an expensive car. I once spent a few days in Houston, Texas, where I met physicians and insurance executives with six-figure annual incomes who felt lower-middle-class because they weren't oil millionaires.

Women drowning in shame starve themselves, wear uncomfortable clothes and shoes, submit to surgery because they have been taught to hate their bodies as not good enough. Men work themselves to the point of collapse, drink too much, or pour out on others — women, gays, Jews, blacks, foreigners — the hatred they feel toward themselves because society has evaluated their earning power and branded them failures. Typically, women turn their anger on themselves; men either turn it on themselves (excessive drinking or other self-inflicted health problems) or find a victim to blame. Shame and guilt teach them to feel disappointed in themselves and drive them to hate anyone who has it better than they do, and to despise anyone who has it worse. And we wonder why people are so lonely and so angry, and why society is so fragmented.

But if shame is a matter of feeling bad for who we *are*, how do we cure shame? The key seems to be having someone you trust and respect give you the message that you deserve to be taken seriously as a person. Ideally we should get that message from our parents, starting on the day we are born. Some children who don't receive that sense of acceptance and worth from their parents may be lucky enough to find a teacher or coach who will give them what they need. When we read stories of people born into the most deprived circumstances (whether financially or emotionally deprived) who go on to lead successful lives, what they all have in common is that somewhere along the way, someone took them in hand and believed in them.

In the moving little book *Random Acts of Kindness*, one anonymous contributor tells her story: "I grew up in what we would now call a dysfunctional family. My parents materially were quite well off, but we lived amidst emotional chaos and confusion in a wealthy suburb of Philadelphia. As with most children, I simply assumed that this was the way it was and the problems, the undercurrents of anger and hostility, were somehow my fault. One day when I was still very young, after a particularly painful and confusing series of interactions with my parents, our maid took me aside to talk to me. She told me that she did not care if it cost her her job, she just could not continue to be a silent observer. She told me that my parents were crazy, that they were acting very badly and not at all like good, loving parents should act toward their children. She told me that I was a good, sweet girl and that the situation was not my fault. . . . It was an incredible gift. Her words gave me the explanation I needed, a way to stop blaming everything on myself." Because shame grows out of our perception of what other people think about us, that message of acceptance and validation is often all we need to conquer shame.

A few years ago, when I was traveling around the country discussing my book *Who Needs God*, dealing with what we gain from being religious, I began to notice something very interesting. In virtually every radio and television studio I visited, after I had spoken about the benefits of being religious, someone — an interviewer, a producer, a cameraman — would take me aside and tell me privately that the most inspiring religious experience he or she had undergone happened not in the church sanctuary on Sunday morning, but in the church basement at an Alcoholics Anonymous gathering or a meeting of some other twelve-step program. There was something authentically religious about what happened to them there. I asked them if they could identify for me exactly what it was that was so helpful, and the word they kept coming up with was "acceptance." The message they heard at the Sunday morning service was that everything they did wrong separated them from God, and only God's grace and generosity could keep them out of hell. The message they got from the Wednesday night twelve-step meeting was "I'm not OK and you're not OK but that's OK." Nothing they did could separate them from God.

A woman told me of going to a support group for compulsive overeaters and confessing to fishing food out of the garbage can after her family had gone to bed. Instead of telling her, "That's sick; you've got a real problem," as her friends did, the other group members responded, "Yes, Jean, we've done that too and we know how terrible we feel when we do that. It will always be a struggle, but you can learn to control yourself."

The group offered not shared strength but shared weakness, "the shared honesty of mutual vulnerability openly acknowledged," the redeeming knowledge that other people — nice, honorable, attractive people — were struggling with the same demons you were, and that you could do for each other what each of you had not been able to do for yourself. As one recovering alcoholic put it, "Therapy offered me explanations; the religiously based support group offered me forgiveness." He was not using the word "forgiveness" in its usual sense; the other members of his AA group were not the people he had hurt with his compulsive drinking. The church-sponsored group was not offering forgiveness for his deeds. It was offering acceptance, forgiveness for his being a flawed, incomplete, imperfect person. It was offering what the synagogue offers its worshippers on the Day of Atonement: the reassurance that if you drop your pretensions and excuses and stand before God naked and vulnerable, if you admit your failures as the first step toward doing something about them, God will not reject you as a flawed specimen. You will still be acceptable in His sight.

The best summary of this religious out-look I have ever seen consisted of four words on a bumper sticker: *God Loves You Anyway*. There is no need to try to fool God, as Adam and Eve tried to do, by blaming others, by claiming that we couldn't help ourselves or we were tricked into it. God knows us too well to be fooled, He knows what we are about, and He loves us anyway. It is not that God doesn't care whether we do right or not. God cares deeply; it is God's caring that invests our moral choices with cosmic significance. But God knows the difference between the deed that is wrong and the person who is not a lost soul for having done wrong. It is more than just a matter of "hating the sin but loving the sinner." God condemns the sin but loves the person who did it too much to brand him a sinner. God may be disappointed in some of the things we do; He is never disappointed in who we are, fallible people struggling with the implications of knowing Good and Evil.

The heroes of the Bible are not perfect people. Their great deeds of faith over-shadow their mistakes, but they all make their share of mistakes because they are human beings, not mythical models of perfection. Abraham sends his wife and son off to starve in the desert, and endangers his other wife by lying about her to save himself. But Abraham is called "the friend of God." Moses repeatedly loses his temper at the people he is supposed to be leading, but Moses is granted an intimacy with God that no other prophet experiences. David commits adultery with a married woman and arranges to have her husband killed, but God loves David as He loves no other Biblical figure. The person who claims to be perfect, without flaw or defect, is claiming to be like God. The person who knows his flaws all too well is open to God's love and God's presence because he realizes he is not God. In the words of authors Ernest Kurtz and Katherine Ketcham, "Imperfection is the wound that lets God in."

It ought to be with a sense of relief, not a sense of compromise and reluctance, that we come to the conclusion that we are not and never will be perfect. We are not settling for mediocrity. We are understanding our humanity, realizing that as human beings, the situations we face are so complex that no one could possibly be expected to get them right all the time. Psychiatrist David Burns writes of a prominent attorney who dreaded losing a case for fear his colleagues would no longer respect him if he were less than perfect. When he finally did lose one, he discovered to his surprise and relief that his colleagues liked him better when he was less perfect, less obsessed with perfection, and more human.

If we are afraid to make a mistake because we have to maintain the pretense of perfection, because we still remember the bitter taste of parental disappointment, of a teacher's criticism or sarcasm, every time we did something wrong, we will never be brave enough to try anything new or anything challenging. We will only do things that are guaranteed to turn out right. We will never learn; we will never grow.

If our parents cannot handle our mistakes, if they have trouble loving us despite our imperfections, it may be because they need us to be perfect to reflect credit on them. If our mates continue to harp on our failures, it may be because they want us to improve and don't know a better way of making that happen. If friends are unforgiving and reject us for our mistakes, it may be because our mistakes touched them at a particularly vulnerable and sensitive place. But God doesn't need us to meet *His* needs, and His expectations of us are more realistic than are those of the people around us. God loves the overweight woman as much as the slender one, the stumbling youngster as much as the athletically gifted one, the frustrated salesman as much as his more successful rival. In fact, God may love them more, because of all the pain they, His children, have endured at the hands of others of His children, and because shame, "the wound that lets God in," has broken through the armor of perfectionist pretense and opened their souls to His presence. God accepts us as we are, and that acceptance is the beginning of the process of healing our shame, because only when we know that we are acceptable and lovable will we be able to change the things we don't like about ourselves.

How can religion help us rise above guilt feelings? How does it silence that voice inside our heads, sometimes a parent's voice, sometimes a teacher's or a clergyman's voice, that says to us, "How could you have done such a thing?"

There are some things we *should* feel guilty about, but the guilt feelings should attach to the deed, not to the doer. The husband who betrays his marriage vows or gambles away his paycheck and leaves his family financially deprived *should* feel guilty. A friend, therapist, or clergyman who accepts his excuse that his wife's nagging drove him to it is doing him no favor. That just permits him to hide from his imperfection, maintain his stance of "I'm fine, I don't have to change, it's all somebody else's fault," and to resist the powers that could help him change and become more fully human. But is he more likely to change if we condemn him as an irresponsible person (rather than condemn what he *did* as irresponsible), or if we tell him instead that inside him is the desire and ability to be a responsible, loving husband and with God's help and the support of friends, that desire and ability can be realized?

I visit a congregant in the hospital. A three-pack-a-day smoker for all of his adult life, he is now dying of lung cancer. He feels guilty for having ruined his health. Do I help him more by saying, "It wasn't your fault; those cigarette ads are so clever they would persuade *anyone* to smoke"? or by saying, "I imagine you must feel pretty bad about yourself and what you've done. But I want to remind you that your wife and kids still love you. They're not angry at you, even if sometimes they're hurting for you, and their fear of the future, comes out sounding like anger. And God still loves you. He hasn't written you off. He knows what you've done to yourself and He loves you anyway. I've come to stand by your bedside and pray with you as a sign and an incarnation of God's love. So if you respect your family's opinion and God's opinion, I want you to never stop loving yourself and thinking of yourself as a good person." My words don't cure his lung cancer, but they may heal the guilt and shame that have been growing malignantly inside him. Reassured of God's love, reassured of his worth as a human being, as a husband, father, and friend, he can now accept my prayers, he can accept his wife's tears and the visits of caring neighbors. It may not help him live longer (though I suspect that believing you deserve to live may help stave off some of the effects of the illness), but it will help him live out his last months feeling loved and cherished.

There are some things we would not feel guilty about if we were totally rational people, but since we are not, we are open to guilt feelings. If we have an overdeveloped sense of responsibility for making things come out right, if we have an exaggerated sense of our power to make things turn out right by doing everything right ourselves, we will make ourselves feel guilty for everything from bad weather to other people's misbehavior. Psychologist Daniel Gottlieb would remind us that "we have no control over another's pain. A lot of guilt comes from the feeling that we have more influence than we really do."

Parents who give birth to a child with a genetic affliction blame themselves, though it was clearly not something they chose to do. They ask themselves, "Did this happen because I drank while pregnant? Because I had sex during the pregnancy? Because I was promiscuous before marriage, or because I resented what the birth of a child would mean for my job, my vacations, my figure?" Parents whose children are injured in an accident berate themselves with thoughts of "If only I hadn't given her permission to go," as if they could have been expected to foresee the future.

Some years ago, I was called on to officiate at two funerals of elderly women in my congregation during the same week in January. I set out to visit both families one afternoon to offer my condolences. At the first home, the eldest son of the deceased woman said to me, "I feel it's my fault that Momma died. I should have insisted on her going to Florida, get her out of this miserable cold weather where you can't even walk outside. If I had done that, she would still be alive today." I tried to console him, and then made my way to the second family's home, where the eldest son said to me, "I feel it's my fault that Mother died. If only I hadn't insisted on her going to Florida. That long plane ride, the abrupt change of climate, was too much for her."

If a story has an unhappy ending, we will berate ourselves endlessly with all the "what-ifs," blaming ourselves for not having made a wiser choice. Guilt is almost always present after a death (because we are still alive and the other one is not, because we made what turned out to be a wrong decision, because a part of us may have been angry at the one who died and may have wished him dead).

But of all the ways in which we can lose someone close to us, guilt is an especially serious problem when the death was a suicide. Suicide is an extraordinarily effective way of making the survivors feel guilty. I know several good books on suicide; all of them share the same flaw. The first half of the book tells us that if we are sufficiently skilled and sensitive, we can pick up warning signals and prevent a suicide. Then the second half goes on to say that if someone we loved took his own life, we shouldn't feel guilty. When a person is determined to kill himself, there is nothing you can do to stop him.

In all likelihood, both statements are correct. A true story: A young man was seeing a therapist twice weekly for treatment of depression. One Friday morning, after their regular session, the therapist said to him, "I don't like what I'm hearing. I'm reluctant to leave you alone over the weekend. I'm afraid you might be tempted to do something to yourself. I'd like you to spend the weekend with my wife and me at our home on Cape Cod." As they were driving to the Cape, the young man asked the therapist to pull over for a moment so that he could go to the bathroom. He started to walk toward the woods by the side of the highway, then suddenly turned and ran into the road, into the path of a speeding truck. He was killed instantly. Here was as close to an ideal situation as anyone could hope for: a trained professional, picking up subtle clues and going out of his way to invite the depressed client to his home. But even that wasn't enough to prevent a person bent on self-destruction from destroying himself.

We can tell people they shouldn't feel guilty; they did everything possible. We can stress that they are not responsible for other people's feelings and actions. But guilt is an irrational feeling. We feel guilty for succeeding ("I don't deserve to be this well off when so many people are less fortunate") and we feel guilty for failing ("You can be anything you want to be if you try hard enough"). We feel guilty for our actions ("It was all my fault"), for our inactions ("Maybe if I had done something more . . ."), and even for our thoughts ("I sinned against my marriage by noticing how attractive that woman at the next table was and fantasizing about what it might lead to if I struck up a conversation with her"). You can't talk someone out of feeling guilty. I know; I've tried hundreds of times. The more you say to them, "You're being unrealistic, there is no need for you to feel guilty about that," the more they hear the message "You're not only guilty, you're unrealistic too." Rather than scold the person for having inappropriate emotions, we should say to them, "I know you feel terrible about what happened, and I hurt for you. But you're a good person and I love you."

If the essence of guilt is the feeling that "I am a bad person and I don't deserve to be loved because of what I have done," we can neutralize that feeling by reassuring the people that we do in fact care about them, not only because *we* are emotionally generous, caring people but because *they* genuinely deserve to be loved. I have often found that support groups, as well as twelve-step programs, are wonderful resources for relieving a person's sense of guilt and restoring his or her sense of self-worth (although men, being notoriously reluctant to admit that they need help, are often hard to persuade to join a support group; when my wife and I attended meetings of the Compassionate Friends after our son died, there were usually three or four bereaved mothers there for every bereaved father). Support groups can often do more than a skilled therapist can, because in a support group, you meet all these good, likable people who have suffered the same misfortune you have, and you begin to realize, "You don't have to be a bad person to have this happen to you." Moreover, in a support group, you take turns helping and being helped, and in the process you learn to see yourself not only as a person burdened by guilt and shame but as a person whose knowledge of guilt and shame has entitled you to help others because you know how they feel and what they need. And at that moment, with that insight, your sense of helplessness and unworthiness begin to lift.

It is unfortunate that so many of us have been brought up to think of religion as the scolding voice that makes us feel guilty. I wish we could learn to see religion as the source of healing and relieving guilt, because so much guilt is irrational (there is no reason for us to feel guilty, but we do and we can't be talked out of it), and religion operates at the nonrational level. Many years ago, an elderly woman in my congregation came in to see me. She told me, "Rabbi, I feel terrible. I did something very bad last week." I waited to hear what terrible sin this woman could have committed. "I went to the cemetery last Thursday to visit my husband's grave."

"Yes, what happened there?"

"Thursday was a Jewish holiday, and I know you're not supposed to go to the cemetery on a holiday. But I was thinking about him and feeling very lonely, so even though I knew it was wrong, I went. And now I feel terrible about what I did."

Because I was a young, inexperienced rabbi, I made the mistake of trying to talk her out of her guilt. I told her that I understood why she wanted to visit her husband's resting place, that that was a valid religious feeling, and that the rule against visiting the cemetery on a holiday was not that important a religious rule. But the more I talked, the more uncomfortable she felt. She felt guilty for what she had done (possibly the cemetery visit had stirred up some buried guilt feelings that had nothing to do with the violation of the holiday), and I wasn't helping her by trying to talk her out of it. Suddenly I had an idea. Irrational guilt feelings required an irrational cure, not a series of rational arguments. I said to her:

"What was the date last Thursday?"

"The seventeenth."

"Give seventeen dollars to charity in your husband's memory, and that will make up for what you did."

The woman brightened visibly. "Oh, Rabbi, thank you. I feel better already."

One of the things religion does best is teach us to cope with the normal guilt that follows a death, and with the appropriate guilt we feel in the wake of our misbehavior. If guilt results from what we have done, the cure is to do other things, better things: random acts of thoughtfulness, giving charity, helping a neighbor. At the rational level, giving charity doesn't undo the selfish or thoughtless thing we did to prompt the guilt feeling in the first place. But at the irrational level, where our souls live, it does introduce us to our better, nobler self. Deed "balances" deed; the voice of healthy pride counters the nagging, disapproving voice of a guilty conscience.

Some years ago, a prominent Boston hospital faced a dilemma. A notorious slumlord wanted to donate a very significant sum of money to name a building in his parents' memory. Some people who knew his reputation and where his money had come from, urged the hospital not to be tainted by his gift. Others, mindful of the hospital's precarious financial condition, urged it to accept. (They may have remembered the exchange in George Bernard Shaw's play *Major Barbara* in which a Salvation Army leader is accused of being willing to accept money from the devil himself. She answers, "Yes, I would, and I'd be happy to get it out of his hands and into mine.") I was among those who argued for acceptance, less out of concern for the hospital than for the donor. If he felt guilty for the way he had accumulated his fortune, I found it appropriate for him to work off his guilt by giving a significant part of that fortune to a worthy cause.

As you have probably noticed over the years, traditional religions often ask us to do things and perform rituals that "don't make sense." At one time or another, we have probably felt impatient with religion for making those apparently meaningless demands. But if these rituals have lasted for centuries, I suspect it must be because they "work" at some nonrational level, helping us in ways we don't understand. When someone close to us dies and we feel guilty for still being alive, for not having been able to do more to save that person, religion gives us ways of making ourselves just uncomfortable enough so that we don't feel we are taking the death lightly. When we have done things we wish we had not done, religion shows us how to balance that wrong deed with a more admirable one. I think of the Jewish custom of sitting *shiva,* staying home for a week after a death, covering all mirrors and sitting on a low, hard bench, and then reciting the mourner's prayer at services daily for a year, or the Roman Catholic system of penances imposed after Confession.

In ancient Israel in biblical times, religion not only defined what was right and what was wrong, what was expected of people. It also gave people something to do when they felt burdened by a sense of falling short of the mark and disappointing God. They would bring a sacrifice, a sin-offering, to God's altar. Its purpose was not to "balance the books" with one good deed to offset every bad one, nor was it to bribe God to overlook their offense. Its purpose was to

85

acquaint the donor with his or her better nature, to let him say to himself, "I would like to be perfect, but I know that I'm not perfect. Sometimes I am weak and thoughtless. But look: sometimes I can be strong and generous and self-disciplined as well. I am not a bad person. I am a person who often does bad things, but more often does good things. And if that's good enough for God, it should be good enough for me." And the sages tell us that in all of Jerusalem, there was no happier person than the man or woman who brought his sin-offering to God's altar and walked away feeling forgiven.

Chapter 4

FATHERS AND SONS, MOTHERS AND DAUGHTERS

When I was a child, I was taught that on Yom Kippur we had to atone for things we had done to hurt other people before we could atone for our offenses against God, and that God would forgive us only when we had forgiven those who had hurt and disappointed us. As I have grown older, I have come to suspect that the first half of that teaching is still valid, but the second half may have it wrong.

I think we have to be forgiven first, we have to learn what it feels like to admit our mistakes and limitations and find out how wonderful it feels not to be rejected for being less than perfect. Once we have that experience, we can offer acceptance to the less-than-perfect people in our lives. And if we don't accept less-than-perfect people into our lives, we will be very lonely, because those are the only kind of people we will find. God would be lonely if He could only love perfect people, and so would we.

Matthew was one of the most promising young people ever to grow up in our congregation. Valedictorian of his high school class, a leader of our synagogue youth group, he went on to a successful academic career at Harvard. He came to see me about six weeks before graduation to fill me in on what had been happening in his life. He would be graduating magna cum laude, his senior thesis had been accepted for publication by a journal that almost never printed articles by undergraduates, and best of all, his favorite professor, his thesis adviser, had offered him a fellowship to work with him on some groundbreaking research.

"Matt," I said to him, "you should be glowing like a man who has just won the lottery. Why do you look so troubled?"

"I'm afraid of accepting his offer. You have to understand, Professor X has been like a father to me, wise and funny and caring and genuinely interested in my career. I have this fantasy of growing up to be like him, to *be* him when I'm his age. I'm afraid that if I work closely with him for the next few years, I'll disappoint him. He'll find out that I'm not really as special as he seems to think I am, and it would hurt me a lot to let him down that way. I'm afraid too that I'll learn some things about him that I don't want to know, and I'll be disappointed in him."

I shook my head and smiled. "Matt, I guarantee you'll be disappointed in each other. We're always disappointed in our parents, and in our parent-substitutes — teachers, clergy, political leaders. They never turn out to be as perfect as we need them to be. And parents are almost always disappointed in their children for the same reason. Why don't you just make up your mind in advance that that's going to happen, and not let that keep you from accepting his offer?"

As children, we want so badly to please our parents. Winning their approval, making them proud and happy means so much to us. As parents, we want our children to succeed, to grow up to be people we can be proud of, to reflect well on us by the way they turn out. In addition to making us proud of them, we want them to love us and admire us. The parent-child relationship is so full of need and expectation on each side that it all too easily slides into unrealistic expectations and inevitable disappointments. Our parents are seldom as wise, and our children are seldom as accomplished, as we think we need them to be.

The relationship between a parent and a child is the most complicated one a person will ever have, even more than between wife and husband. When Jungian analysts deal with a patient who has a problem letting his or her emotions out, they have an exercise in which the patient imagines some important person in his past sitting in a chair in front of him, and says all the things to the empty chair that he has never been able to say to the actual person. Analysts tell me that nine out of ten patients imagine a parent in the chair rather than a spouse, boss, child, or friend.

An interesting detail of Jewish law decrees that a person who sustains the loss of a family member remain in a state of mourning for thirty days for a husband or wife, brother, sister, or child. But for a parent, one is a mourner for just under a year, because when a parent dies, you lose not one but several relationships: the powerful, life-sustaining parent of your early years, the person who tried to shape and control you when you were growing up, the companion of your adult years, and if the parent lives long enough to reverse roles, the dependent, vulnerable elderly person. And there tends to be more unfinished business, more unresolved conflicts in these multiple relationships with our parents than in any of our other relationships. It has been suspected by many authorities that often the problems between husband and wife in a marriage stem from unresolved conflicts with one or both sets of parents.

Sophocles' play *Oedipus Rex* is considered the greatest of the Greek tragedies. Shakespeare's *Hamlet* is considered the greatest play of all time. Dostoyevski's *The Brothers Karamazov* is generally thought to be the finest psychological novel ever written. What is fascinating is that they are all about the same subject, a man trying to come to terms with his father's violent death. Freud's interpretation of *Hamlet* is that Hamlet had trouble avenging his father's murder because part of him identified so strongly with what his uncle had done, murdering the father and marrying the mother.

We respond to plays and novels on that theme because they touch the dark corners of our soul, where we feel anger at our parents and try to hide that anger because we also love them, need them, and feel grateful to them. And parents also feel anger at their children; think of the twenty-second chapter of Genesis, in which Abraham hears God's voice telling him to offer up his son, Isaac, as a sacrifice. Could that strange story somehow reflect the repressed wish of a parent to do away with a child who has disappointed him?

Why the anger? Because we need each other so much and we are so disappointed when the other cannot meet those needs. Because children want their parents to protect them from harm, and parents can't always protect them. Sigmund Freud's biographer tells the story of how, when Freud was a child, he was walking with his father in the streets of Vienna when an anti-Semitic bully knocked the father's fur hat off his head and said, "Jew, walk in the gutter." Freud never forgot that moment of seeing his father powerless and humiliated.

Children need parents who will let them grow up to be themselves, but parents often have personal agendas they try to impose on their children. It may be that parents count on their children for the blessing of vicarious immortality, that something of them will live on beyond their lifespan, not only their biological DNA but their names, their values, their identity, and children often insist on going their own way in the choice of a mate or a career. Or it may be that parents want their children to reflect credit on them, and feel that every flaw in a child reflects badly on their parenting (one recalls Garrison Keillor's quip about his home town where all the students are above average), while children want and need the freedom to make mistakes and learn from those mistakes.

Giving birth to a child, conceiving and nurturing a brand new human life inside of you, is probably the most creative thing a woman will ever do. (I have long suspected that the great lengths men go to to "make a name for themselves," have a building or company named after them, write books or symphonies, merit a paragraph in the encyclopedia, are in fact efforts to compensate for not being able to give birth to a child.) When Eve gives birth to the first child ever born to a human parent, she says, "I have gotten a person with God" (meaning "with the help of God" or perhaps "just like God"). Eve, who was tempted to be like God by acquiring the knowledge of good and evil, now has become like God by doing something that only God had previously done, fashioning a human being. She names him Cain, which the Bible relates to the Hebrew verb *canah*, "to acquire," so that Eve's words can be read to mean "I have acquired a person, he belongs to me."

At best, children represent a fresh start, an opportunity to begin again with the benefit of the experience of previous generations but without the burden of their scars and mistakes. Sometimes, children are seen as an opportunity for the parents to live their lives over again, in the hope of getting it right this time. So the father who wanted to be an athlete, but never was, pushes his child in that direction and gets into shouting arguments with the Little League coach over his eight-year-old son's playing time. And the mother who was hurt by not being sought after for dates in high school has her daughter putting on makeup and wearing a training bra at age eleven. Like Eve, they respond to parenthood by saying, "I have acquired a person; I am like God, I will shape him or her into something wondrous and everyone will admire me for it," forgetting that even God's creatures didn't turn out the way He hoped they would.

It can be amusing to listen to young mothers in a playground scoring points by comparing the ages at which their toddlers reached certain milestones, or seeing a father in the stands taking a game more seriously than his child on the field is doing. It can be amusing to see so many cars (including my own) displaying stickers that brag about where our children go to college. But beyond a certain point, this quest to have your children reflect credit on you by their achievements stops being amusing and can become destructive. It can mean pushing children into music or ballet lessons for which they have neither interest nor talent, and telling them that if they would only apply themselves, they would excel, with the possible result that they will learn to think of themselves as failures for not possessing unusual talent. (Only years later, when it's too late to undo those childhood feelings, will they learn that athletic and musical talent is inherited from parents.) It can mean forcing a career choice, or interfering with a romance, for reasons which meet the parents' needs more than the child's. It can create a situation in which several generations live by proxy, living someone else's life plan and waiting for someone to come along and live yours: "I sacrificed my dreams to make my parents happy, and I expect you to sacrifice yours to make me happy. If you do, your reward will be the right to demand that your children sacrifice their dreams to make you happy." Do we really want to live like that?

This pattern of expecting children to validate one's worth as a parent can become most destructive when people find themselves parents of a handicapped or retarded child. If what you look forward to with the birth of a child is that he or she will grow up to be perfect or near-perfect and show the world what a perfect or near-perfect parent you are, how will you respond to a child who is severely limited from birth? Such children need a lot of love and respond beautifully to love. They can be happy, outgoing, and affectionate. What they can't be is perfect. They will be loving and lovable, but they won't be valedictorians, star athletes, or homecoming queens. I have seen too many parents angry at children for being born handicapped or intellectually limited, because that shattered the parent's misplaced dreams.

I confess that I have never liked or understood the story in chapter 22 of the Book of Genesis, where God commands Abraham to sacrifice his son, Isaac, born to him after many years of childlessness, and then intervenes to stop it at the last moment. I never liked the way it portrayed God, making such an outrageous demand, or the way it portrayed Abraham, so ready to obey it. But some years ago, I read an article by a physician suggesting that Isaac may have been a retarded child. He shares many of the traits of the retarded. He was born to older parents. He periodically gets into trouble by not understanding the consequences of his actions. He is the only man in all the Bible whose parents worry about his getting married, and ends up marrying a woman whose outstanding quality is her kindness. If that theory is correct, the doctor wrote, maybe that is why Abraham thought he heard the voice of God telling him to slay his son, as many societies in the ancient world did to imperfect children. And God's intervening would then represent His proclaiming to Abraham that even such a child is fashioned in God's image, that even such a life is holy, that a child is born to grow to be himself, and not to be used to fill in the blank spaces in a parent's ego.

James Wilkes writes of the reaction of parents upon learning that their son or daughter is gay. "The parents need help to see that they had an illusion of their idealized child, an illusion-child made in their image. Once they understand that they had this illusion, they need help to let that illusion die. The death of that illusion and the bringing to life of the love they have for the real child is clearly an act of courage. . . . The real child will come to life only when the illusory child dies."

I can imagine how painful it is for parents to accept the idea that their son or daughter will never marry or give them grandchildren because he or she is gay. They can respond with anger, or they can respond with guilt ("What did we do wrong?"). And in fortunate instances, they can respond by giving up their idealized dreams and by supporting their children in their struggle to be who they have to be, not who the parents need them to be.

There are two things wrong with expecting your children to give your life meaning by excelling. The first is that it is a very unreliable way of achieving satisfaction. I have heard college basketball coaches complain that their chances of keeping their jobs depend on some eighteen-year-old freshman making his foul shots at the end of a close game. How much more insecure must a father or mother be whose happiness depends on a ten-year-old child's getting straight A's or an adolescent son or daughter's being polite rather than rebellious?

But the real problem with this approach is that it asks more of a young child than is reasonable. It gives children more power over us than is healthy for them. A child has enough to do just growing up to be herself; to ask her to invest her parents' lives, which would otherwise be meaningless, with meaning is terribly unfair. I have seen young children asked, implicitly or explicitly, to lend order to a family situation rendered chaotic by alcoholism or mental illness, to take responsibility in a family where a parent has died, to maintain peace between a quarreling husband and wife. How many parents ask their daughters, "Why can't you marry a rich man?" How many inner city parents ask their sons, "Why can't you be a basketball star and earn millions of dollars and buy your parents a new home, like all the players I read about?" Needless to say, those are unrealistic expectations born of desperation, but too many impressionable youngsters, desperately wanting to please their parents, grow up feeling they let their parents down by not reaching those goals. Such demands inevitably distort children, robbing them of their childhood. Some children emerge strengthened by the experience, some are broken by it. But whatever the outcome, it is too much of a burden to put on such young and unformed shoulders.

The amount of harm a child can do to a parent is limited. They can embarrass us, but only if we have invested our reputations in how they turn out. They can disappoint us, but that probably hurts them more than it hurts us. They want so badly to please us.

But parents can harm their children much

more seriously. We harm them not only with physical and emotional violence. We harm them with unrealistic expectations. (A colleague of mine says that "being disappointed" is a uniquely middle-class form of child abuse.) And we harm them by not modeling an adult lifestyle for them, an approach that includes a willingness to make and admit mistakes and learn from them rather than always insisting that we are right. Children need to admire their parents. And one of the things we should teach our children to admire about us is our willingness to say, "I'm sorry," "I was wrong about that," "I don't know." I can remember times I had to tell my children that I had been wrong about something, how fearful I was that they would lose respect for me because of that admission, and how astonished I was to find that they loved me all the more for being willing to say that. They needed to hear that from me. They needed to be assured of my integrity more than of my perfection.

If we try to teach our children to see us as perfect, they will be terribly disappointed when our imperfections emerge, as they inevitably do. But if we teach them to see us as people trying to grow by learning from our mistakes, then we make it easier for them to see their own mistakes and failures as lessons to be learned from, rather than badges of shame and incompetence.

For years, I have tried to understand why J. D. Salinger's novel *Catcher in the Rye* has become a cult classic for so many young people. It catches the sensitivity and idealism of young people, which is not always recognized by their elders, and it skewers the "phoniness" of the adult world. The hero of the novel, Holden Caulfield, is constantly dismissing people as "phonies." As you may recall from your own adolescence or that of your children, spotting the hypocrisy of parents and other authority figures is a major preoccupation of teenagers. Why hypocrisy, of all the sins to which the human soul is prone? I suspect young people react so strongly to it because it is an issue for them. They are bothered by the inconsistencies they find in themselves, brave one day and hiding behind lies the next, cruel to a friend in the morning and kind in the afternoon. Just as they admire the athlete excessively because he has gained control over his body while they are having so much trouble with theirs, they admire the person who has it "together," who can live consistently by the same values day in and day out (even as we will say admiringly of someone who holds consistent but extreme political views, "I don't agree with him, but at least you know where he stands"). Teenagers are disproportionately upset by their parents' inconsistencies because a part of them has been hoping fervently, "By the time I get to be that age, I'll have solved the problem. I'll know who I am and what I stand for." They are more than disappointed, they are frightened when they learn from their parents' behavior that this is still an issue for adults.

How do we respond to our children's accusing us of inconsistency? We can respond as Adam did in the Garden of Eden, claiming perfection, denying our mistakes, looking for someone else to blame, or not recognizing the right of anyone to judge us. Or we can drop the fig leaf of perfection and reveal ourselves as human beings doing our best, getting some things right and others wrong as we continue to grow and struggle. Integrity is not something that grownups have and adolescents can aspire to. Integrity is something that all of us, at all ages, are constantly striving for.

It can be said of young children, as it has been said of the elderly, that they need so little from us but they need that little so much. They need permission to make mistakes and not be called "bad" for it. We gave them that permission when they were growing physically. When our children were not quite a year old and just starting to walk, they would take a tentative step or two and fall down. We didn't scold them for being clumsy. We praised them for their efforts to do something new, and assured them that with practice they would get better at it. We owe them the same praise and the same patience with their moral growth.

And children need to know that they are loved and trusted, because sometimes they know themselves and their shortcomings so well that they can't be sure they are lovable and trustworthy, and because sometimes we forget or find it emotionally hard to tell them.

I know a man, a successful business executive, who works twelve hours a day, six days a week, to make his business even more successful than it already is. He doesn't have to do it. He is financially secure; his company will certainly continue to be successful for the foreseeable future. He could easily spend more time on his seldom-used yacht, at his vacation home, or on the golf course. Why does he continue to work so hard? Because his father was a successful businessman, and my friend lives for the day when he will hear his father tell him, "I'm proud of you; you're as good as I ever was." My friend wears himself out to earn that compliment, but he will never hear it. His father has been dead for fifteen years.

My friend has never been able to get over the fact that when he was a child, he was never sure how much his father loved him. He was taught that love had to be earned: "You'll have to do better than that if you expect me to be satisfied." My friend's father was feared and respected in the business community, and probably used that approach to get results from his employees, demanding much and praising so rarely that a compliment from the "old man" was a medal of honor. And apparently he was the same person at home. It worked at the office. People worked harder to avoid his criticism and maybe even earn his praise. And in a sense it "worked" at home. His children were all driven to succeed in school and in their professions. But at what cost? If I could bring my friend's father back from the dead for long enough to ask him two questions, "If you had to choose one, would you rather have been a successful businessman or a successful father? Would you rather have raised children to make good livings or to be good people?" I suspect his eyes would fill with tears and that would give me my answer before a word was spoken. Maybe he would blame his own father or the circumstances of his growing up. Maybe he would deny my premise that you can't have both. (Of course you can have both if you're smart enough and lucky enough, but my friend's unscratchable itch for parental approval reminds me how hard that is to do.)

I try to tell my friend that the problem was with his father, not with him. His father never said, "I love you," because the father was an emotionally constricted man, not because the son wasn't lovable. I point out to him that so many hundreds of people inside and outside the industry have praised his business acumen, that his balance sheet, his market share, his wall full of plaques and awards testify to his achievement, and what does he still have to prove? But none of that is enough to fill the emptiness represented by the words he never heard from his father.

I have seen what happens when a man brings his son (and in recent years, his daughter) into the business he has built up over the years, sometimes to give his child a head start on the road to success, sometimes as a way of ensuring that his name and the business he created will live on after his death. When it works, it can be wonderful. But so often, these arrangements start out with high hopes and deteriorate into friction and often heartbreak. I can't count the number of times I have been asked to counsel either a father or a son in a business relationship, sometimes because the son simply didn't have the business skills the father did, sometimes because the son (armed with an MBA) wanted to change things and the aging father insisted on holding on to the decision-making power. Freud once wrote, "Every man is jealous of another man's success," while the sages of the Talmud, seventeen centuries earlier, put it, "Every man is jealous of another man's success except a father of his son and a teacher of his pupil." I used to think that the Talmud understood human nature better than Freud did, but I have seen so many cases of elderly fathers, sometimes extremely successful ones, jealous of a son who was younger, earning more money, and getting the admiration which was once theirs, that I wonder if Freud's darker view of human nature might not be the truer one.

There is a strange passage in the Bible, in the nineteenth chapter of the First Book of Kings. The prophet Elijah has grown discouraged by the tendency of the Israelites to abandon their faith in God and serve idols. He has spent a lifetime trying to get them to shun idolatry, but they keep returning to it. Depressed, he runs to the desert, all the way to Mount Sinai, where God and Israel first entered into a covenant. He throws himself on the ground and tells God that he feels like a failure and wants to die because "I am no better than my fathers." God responds in a still, small voice, giving Elijah specific things to do to save the situation. But I have always been struck by that sentence "I am no better than my fathers." We all seem to have this need to be better than our parents. It would seem to represent a way of surpassing them and pleasing them at the same time.

I have a theory that many men and women who grew up with strong, successful fathers end up doing professionally what their fathers did as a hobby or volunteer work (my father was a successful businessman who was active in his synagogue; I became a rabbi), or will do as a sideline what their father did for a living (the teacher's child who goes on to become a successful lawyer or entrepreneur finds time to teach a course at the local community college). It is a way of following in the father's footsteps without having to compete with him head-to-head, without the danger of not being as good or the risk of surpassing him.

I have often suspected that one of the reasons children of great men grow up to be nonentities is not just that their parents neglected them in the pursuit of greatness, but because a great man doesn't leave his children much room to surpass him. In recent years, I have heard many grown children of successful businessmen tell me, "I will probably never make as much money as my father made. I will probably not raise my family in as nice a house as I grew up in. But I'll have my head on straight. I won't be a slave to business. I won't bring work home on weekends. I'll have a better sense of what's really important than my parents had." These young people, feeling unable to compete with their parents in terms of material success, have redefined success in the one way that lets them feel "better than my father."

If we, at great effort, maintain a posture of perfection and if our children believe and admire us (because they want to believe and admire us), we leave them little room to surpass us and little hope of doing so. But if we leave them instead a sense of our imperfect humanity and an unfinished agenda (as King David left it for his son Solomon to build the Temple, thereby achieving something his immensely successful father could never do), then instead of casting a shadow over them and stunting their growth, we leave them a space in which they can grow and flourish.

With some effort and some practice, we can learn to accept the innocent mistakes our parents made. We can come to see them as emotionally limited, and as limited in their psychological insights, and we can understand why they did the things they did. But what about parents whose mistakes were less innocent and less forgivable?

A woman came up to me after services one Sabbath and asked if she could speak to me. She told me that she had just learned that her father was dying of cancer and had no more than a month or two to live. I anticipated her asking me about making funeral arrangements and about the details of sitting *shiva*, the Jewish memorial week following a death. I wasn't prepared for what she really needed to talk about.

"I hate my father," she told me. "I won't be sorry when he dies, and I don't want to have to pretend that I am. He left the family when I was nine years old. It turned out that he had had a number of girlfriends over the years and was planning to marry his latest one. My mom had to work two jobs to support us. He showed no interest in my high school or college graduation. When I got married, he refused to pay for any of the wedding unless I let him walk me down the aisle, and when I told him I couldn't handle that, he didn't even attend. That was more than ten years ago, and I haven't spoken to him since then. Thursday, his second wife called me to tell me he was dying. Rabbi, can you give me any reason why I should mourn for a man like that, why I should go to the funeral or say *kaddish* for him?"

I told her, "First of all, if you go to the funeral and decide afterward that you made a mistake, that you would have been better off not going, that's just a mistake and you'll get over it quickly enough. But if you stay away from the funeral and afterward realize that you should have gone, I'm afraid you'll carry the burden of that guilt for a much longer time. But more importantly, this is your opportunity to mourn the father you never had. From what you tell me, I can't ask you to grieve for your real father who is dying. But why not take this opportunity to grieve for the father you should have had but didn't? When he was alive, what you felt was anger, and I can understand why. Once he is dead, let yourself feel sadness for the person he wasn't able to be, for the absence of a father when you were growing up, for the empty space at your wedding and all those other family occasions. When you recite the *kaddish*, the mourner's prayer, you won't be expressing sadness that he died. You'll be expressing and coming to terms with your sadness that he couldn't be a father to you even when he was alive, and now that he's gone, there is no longer even the possibility of his making it up to you."

She attended the funeral, and told me afterward that she felt very confused emotionally during the service. She was not sure what she was feeling, but to her surprise she wasn't feeling angry. She attended services weekly for about a month and a half and then stopped, which I took as a healthy sign that she was no longer filled with anger and resentment toward a man who was no longer alive and a situation that could not be changed.

Even under less extreme circumstances, the vulnerability and neediness of an aging, ill, or dying parent forces an adult child to confront his or her anger toward that parent, anger that may be decades old and perhaps unfair but is there nonetheless. The vulnerability of a sick, dying father, his pleading with us to spend more time with him, may move us to recall times when he wasn't there for us, too busy with work or friends to see us in a high school play, or the times he was physically there but emotionally unavailable. The actress Lynn Redgrave recalls how, as a child, she found her father's diary, eagerly opened it to the day she was born, and was crushed to find the diary contained no mention of her birth, only news of the play he was rehearsing and the German air raids over London. Only after his death was she able to come to terms with his emotional remoteness, his inability to feel and express what she wanted and needed him to, and learn to see it as a flaw in him, not in her.

Many of us carry memories of times we asked for something and were refused. Our parents may well have been right to say no to us, or they may have been wrong for perfectly honorable and understandable reasons. But it left a scar, causing us to feel confused and ambivalent years later when our parents in their time of need ask us for something.

I see this all too often when a parent is terminally ill and the doctors ask the family's permission to withhold extraordinary measures. In effect, they are asking the child to let Momma or Poppa die. How does a grown child make such a decision? How does she sort out in her own mind whether the decision not to use extraordinary treatment is motivated by not wanting to prolong the parent's suffering, by a reluctance to spend the money for it when it won't do any good, by the return of a repressed wish buried in childhood to get even with the parents and wish them dead, or simply a weariness at having to drive to the hospital and find parking every day? That is why I recommend that the decision not be left up to the children but that the doctors, perhaps in consultation with family clergy, say to the family (as my father's doctors said to my brother and me when the time came), "This is what we recommend; is that all right with you?" That way, the children are not left out of the decision-making process, but are not saddled with the burden and subsequent guilt of making that terrible decision.

When a parent dies, even a parent whom we loved and with whom we got along, we not only grieve for the fact that they will no longer be with us to share birthdays and graduations. We also grieve for the fact that, if there were words that should have been spoken and weren't spoken, now they never will be. If we longed for their approval and they weren't able to put it into words because of the kind of people they were, now we will never hear those words. If we had in mind to apologize to them for having hurt them with the excesses of our adolescence and kept putting it off because it was hard to do, because we said to ourselves, "It was so long ago, why bring it up again now?" we realize now that we will never have the chance. That is why therapists often ask patients mourning a parent to "write a letter to the deceased parent, saying all the things you wish you had said in his or her lifetime, and then write a letter to yourself in the deceased parent's name, saying all the things you wish they had said to you when they were alive." And that is why all religions give us elaborate customs of grieving and mourning for a parent, as an act of reconciliation for all the inevitable disappointments on both sides of the relationship.

Several people have told me that they heard bestselling author John Bradshaw say on television that virtually all families are dysfunctional families. But Bradshaw didn't say exactly that. He had quoted another psychologist as saying that 96 percent of families are dysfunctional, and he quickly went on to add that that number was not meant to be taken literally. It was merely an attention-getter.

I find it interesting that so many people heard what they wanted to hear: a national authority telling them that they had problems because their parents had messed them up. They welcomed that pronouncement. They thought it relieved them of responsibility. Their problems were their parents' fault, not theirs. But in fact, as I will try to show, that point of view (with which I strenuously disagree) actually adds to their burden of responsibility.

Ninety-six to 100 percent of all families are dysfunctional only if we define dysfunctional as being anything less than perfect. If every parent who ever makes a mistake is a dysfunctional parent because that mistake leaves its mark on us, then indeed we all come from dysfunctional homes. When it comes to designing a spaceship or building a bridge, one imperfection can make the whole project worthless. But raising a child to be a human being is so much more complicated than building a space shuttle that a zero tolerance for error is simply unrealistic. Fortunately children are resilient enough to survive most of our mistakes, especially if they occur against a background of love and support, free of the expectations of perfection on our part or theirs.

There are no perfect families. There are truly dysfunctional families, racked by alcoholism, incest, and violence, but fortunately there are relatively few such households. And then there are the rest of us, raised in homes in which loving, well-intentioned parents, themselves the products of well-intentioned but flawed parents, try to do their best with us and get some things right and some things wrong.

Those people who (mis)quoted Bradshaw to me were saying that they had the right to expect perfection from their parents, and were entitled today to resent their parents for not having gotten it totally right. But are those same people prepared to tell their own children, "You have the right to expect me to be perfect, to know all the answers, always to be available, never distracted"? And are they prepared to live up to the terms of that contract? I suspect that the issue of dysfunctional parenting being responsible for flawed people looks different when we become parents and realize what a hard job it is. (Wasn't that every mother's curse when they were upset with us? "May you one day have a child just like you.")

In Marian Wright Edelman's bestselling book *The Measure of Our Success*, she has a chapter entitled "A Letter to My Sons." It includes the following remarkable paragraph:

"I seek your forgiveness for all the times I talked when I should have listened; got angry when I should have been patient; acted when I should have waited; feared when I should have been delighted; scolded when I should have encouraged; criticized when I should have complimented; said no when I should have said yes and said yes when I should have said no. I did not know a whole lot about parenting or how to ask for help. I often tried too hard and wanted and demanded so much, and mistakenly sometimes tried to mold you into my image of what I wanted you to be rather than discovering and nourishing you as you emerged and grew."

Let me tell you two things about that paragraph. First, I believe that 90 percent of parents feel that way (and unlike Bradshaw, I mean that number to be taken literally). I know I do. Outwardly we may defend and justify ourselves as having been right, out of a misplaced notion that we would be better parents if we were seen as perfect. But in our hearts lie buried the regrets of all the things we wish we had done differently. Every line of Ms. Edelman's letter brings memories of moments in my children's lives that I wish I had back to do over again and do it right this time: days when I invested too much of my soul in my work and had too little left when I came home; times when I took my children's words at face value and gave their questions a superficial, glib response when a little probing would have revealed the need or the fear behind the innocent question.

Second, very few parents are brave enough to take off the armor of parental expertise and reveal their vulnerability by saying that to their children. I don't know if even Marian Wright Edelman was brave enough to say it out loud to her sons. She may have written it in her book instead (which, it occurs to me, is what I am doing as well).

The hardest part of writing this chapter for me was facing up to my memories of my own parents, now both deceased, and the buried resentments I still carry toward them for the mistakes they made. They were good, kind, loving people who set a splendid example for me in many ways, but they were not perfect. They made their share of mistakes. If there were such a thing as parental malpractice suits, I suspect I could have found some unscrupulous lawyer to take the evidence and plead my case.

My parents taught me, by precept and example, to take education seriously, to be honest and charitable, to be religiously committed yet respectful of people with different religions or no religion. I am grateful to them for all of that. I have memories of my father sending money to needy relatives overseas, welcoming the first black family onto our block, indignantly rejecting suggestions that he falsify his tax returns in ways that would probably never be detected, and I am pleased when I find those same qualities in myself. But at the same time, my father had some less admirable qualities — he could be impatient and condescending, he could drive us crazy by hiding behind a newspaper and detaching himself from the other people in a room, and he never appreciated having these faults pointed out to him — and it annoys me terribly when I catch myself acting like him and remember having vowed when I was younger, "I'll never be like that when I grow up."

My parents, like most of their friends, were European-born, middle-class Jews who were caught up in a benignly competitive crowd in which you scored bragging rights through your children's educational and professional achievements. I suspect that they (perhaps unconsciously) had the envy of their friends in mind as much as my well-being when they pushed me through school so that I was in college by age sixteen and in a demanding graduate program by the time I was twenty. (My father lived long enough to see me attain a national reputation as an author and lecturer, and since none of his friends' children ever achieved as much, I guess that means he "won.") I would probably have benefited from a more normal education, but I benefited from my parents in so many ways that I know my resentments are unreasonable. Yet for whatever reasons, I find many years after the fact that their minor mistakes annoy me more than their major virtues gratify me. Maybe it is because I admired them so much that I wanted them to be perfect. But having survived their mistakes, I guess I should be glad that they weren't. Who would really want to be the child of perfect parents?

Thomas Moore writes in his book *Soul Mates*, "Our task as adults then might be to search for whatever it takes to forgive our parents for being imperfect. In some families, that imperfection will be slight, in others severe, but in any case we have to deal with evil and suffering in our own lives without benefit of a scapegoat. In fact, our lives would be all the richer if we could let go of the excuse of parental failure. . . . Thinking negatively and pathologically about the family distances us from family members and we lose the opportunity to be enriched by them."

Eve, who never had a mother to provide her with a role model, tried to "own" her children, hoping that they would get it right and make up for her mistakes. The results were disheartening. One child was killed by his brother, who then became a fugitive, before she and Adam could start over again with lessened expectations. In a sense, the Bible is a chronicle of good people being bad parents, with Abraham banishing one of his sons and almost murdering the other, with Isaac, Rebecca, and Jacob all favoring one child over another and causing problems in the family by doing so, with Jacob's sons being murderously jealous of their brother Joseph. Yet those "dysfunctional" families produced people who, for all their scars and traumas, laid the foundations for Western culture.

Marian Wright Edelman asks her children to forgive her. Thomas Moore calls on us to forgive our parents. I am not sure forgiveness is the right word. Maybe when we are young adults, forgiveness is the appropriate currency. By the time we become parents ourselves, the coinage is likely to be not forgiveness but understanding and appreciation, because we will then have made the same mistakes ourselves and come to understand how unreasonable it was to expect perfection from a human parent.

Victoria Farnsworth has written, "Not until I became a mother did I understand how much my mother had sacrificed for me. Not until I became a mother did I feel how hurt my mother was when I disobeyed. Not until I became a mother did I know how proud my mother was when I achieved. Not until I became a mother did I realize how much my mother loved me."

When we liberate ourselves from the myth that God will love us only if we are perfect, then we will no longer feel that we need to be parents of perfect children to be admired, or children of perfect parents to survive and succeed.

I don't find it necessary to forgive my parents for the mistakes they made. It is no sin to be human. They were amateurs in a demanding game where even experts can't always get it right. Beyond forgiveness, I love and admire them for all the good things they did, and I hope I have shown that love and admiration in the way they would have wanted me to, by passing on many of those good qualities to my own daughter, who I pray will find herself inclined to understand and to admire me.

Chapter 5

CHOOSING HAPPINESS OVER RIGHTEOUSNESS

In an earlier chapter, when I summarized the biblical story of the Creation leading up to that primal act of disobedience, I described God fashioning a mate for Adam by taking one of his ribs and then added "(or maybe it wasn't a rib)." The time has come to explain that parenthetical comment. The Hebrew word used in the narrative is *tsela,* which often means "rib," and by the time of the emergence of Christianity, both Jews and Christians were familiar with the story of God's fashioning Eve from Adam's rib. But more often the word *tsela* means "side," as it does in Exodus 26:26 and many other places, and I am inclined to agree with the Bible scholars who find in the second chapter of Genesis the biblical parallel to a myth found in Greek and Hindu sources, and in many other ancient cultures. It would read as follows:

As the climax of Creation, God fashioned

a two-sided human being, one side of which was male and one side female. "Male and female He created them" (Gen. 1:27). When this androgynous creature could find no suitable mate among all the animals, God caused it to fall asleep and surgically separated one *side* from the other, leaving a masculine human being and a feminine human being, who were then suitable mates for each other. That is why the story of the creation of Eve concludes with the words "Therefore shall a man leave his father and mother and cleave unto his wife, *and they shall become one flesh*" (Gen. 2:24). That is, when man and woman come together, they restore the sense of unity they had at the moment of their original creation.

(We find the same story in Plato's *Symposium*, except that in the Greek version, some of the original double-creatures were two males, explaining why some men seek male partners.)

The implications of taking that one word in its meaning of "side" rather than "rib" are numerous and significant. For one thing, it makes Eve a full partner in Creation rather than an afterthought. More interestingly, it gives marriage a meaning for humans far beyond what it can have for other creatures. It is more than a way of bringing children into the world and continuing the species. It is more than a way of validating our ability to attract someone of the opposite sex (a trait we share with a number of other animal species, where the males compete for the most attractive females). Human beings marry to find wholeness, to make themselves complete. The deepest reason for getting married is not to satisfy ourselves sexually or psychologically, nor is it to give us the opportunity to please and satisfy another person. This new reading of the story of the creation of the first human beings would tell us that the purpose of marriage is to create a new entity, a single being made up of two formerly separate individuals, each supplying what the other lacks. That is why divorce, however legally accessible and socially acceptable, and however necessary in individual cases, is always such a wrenching experience. It represents the surgical separation of two souls that had been fused. Many of the worst moments of my thirty years as a rabbi occurred when I became involved in the quarrels of a couple who had once loved each other and no longer did. As a friend of mine once told me, "I never knew how angry I could get until I got married." It is an immense act of courage to love someone, to make yourself vulnerable by caring for someone so much that they can hurt you in ways that strangers can't, and they know how to hurt you with a clarity that outsiders can never have. I worry that people who don't grieve for a failed marriage, who say, "It was never right from the beginning, I should have done it sooner," are like people who don't mourn at a funeral. They are burying their feelings of sadness, and will have to face up to them somewhere down the line.

Such a union, when it works, can provide us with the most sublime feeling many of us will ever know, the sense of transcending our isolation in the world and finding a new sense of wholeness, a sense of having the empty places in our lives filled. When it doesn't work, we feel more than disappointed. We feel betrayed. We expected the other person to make everything right, to make our problems vanish, and it turns out that they brought new problems of their own into the mix.

One of the basic needs of every human being is the need to be loved, to have our wishes and feelings taken seriously, to be validated as people who matter. Birthday parties help fill that need, as does seeing our name or picture in the newspaper. Infants need love from their parents as surely as they need food and warmth, and the consequences are dire if they don't get it. And as we outgrow our dependence on our parents, we begin the search for someone who will cherish us in a unique and intimate way.

When we are young, our ability to form relationships with someone of the opposite sex is the way we establish the "market value" of our attractiveness. Boyfriends and girlfriends are the mirror in which we evaluate our being attractive and lovable. Often, young men seek "trophy" girlfriends and later "trophy" wives, partners sought not for their personal qualities but for their ability to impress others with the man's ability to win such a desirable companion. Young women vie for the right to be seen with the most sought-after male student, and later to marry the man other women will envy her for. Young girls obsess over having a boyfriend, keeping a boyfriend, losing a boyfriend to their best friend, and wondering despondently if life is worth living without one, while young men perspire nervously as they prepare to call a girl for a date and risk being rejected. And those of us who can't attract the most desirable partners are constantly reminded in subtle and not-so-subtle ways that because of our limitations, we had to settle for "second best."

To a greater or lesser extent, we never entirely outgrow that outlook. A part of us keeps thinking that our worth as a human being will be determined by the desirability of the mate we are able to attract. "If I can get him/her to love me, I must be pretty wonderful. If I have to settle for the boy-friend/girlfriend that nobody else is interested in, that says something about me as well."

Several years ago, *Boston* magazine, an upscale monthly publication in the city near my home, ran an article on the problems of successful businesswomen in finding suitable husbands. In the course of that article, we were introduced to the woman who came to be known as the "season ticket lady." A female business executive was interviewed about her efforts to meet men as bright, as driven, as successful as she was. She described how she finally met a charming, thoughtful, successful man who seemed to like her as well. After several dates and a growing sense of mutual affection, she felt serious enough about the relationship to ask him if he shared her enthusiastic love for ballet. He answered, "No, but I'm willing to learn." She broke off the relationship, saying, "I don't want somebody who's willing to learn about ballet. I want someone who has season tickets."

That line generated a landslide of letters to the magazine from people trying to psychoanalyze that woman on the basis of one sentence. Some accused her of a fear of intimacy, leading her to break off relationships before they led anywhere. Some thought she suffered from low self-esteem and rejected people before they had a chance to reject her. My suspicion was that the culprit responsible for souring that romance was our old familiar enemy, the quest for perfection. I suspect her thinking process may have been, "At work, I have to project an image of perfection. Because I'm a woman in a high-stress job, I have to maintain a sense of being in control, of getting everything right. If I could find a perfect husband, that would enhance my image of being a perfect woman, a woman who can do everything and do it well. If I have to settle for a flawed, imperfect husband, a man lacking something essential (like season tickets to the ballet?), that might be seen as testifying to a flaw, a lack of perfection in me." The result for people like that is either that they keep on looking, finding reasons to disqualify everyone who comes along, or else they persuade themselves that their current beau is in fact perfect for them, and then react with fury and sorrow when they find out that he isn't something he never claimed to be.

Nathaniel Hawthorne wrote a short story, "The Birthmark," about a man who married a beautiful woman who had a small birthmark on her left cheek. She had always thought of it as a beauty spot, but for him, it spoiled her appearance. It kept her from being perfect. He became so obsessed with the birthmark that it became all he could see. He could no longer see her beauty; he could only focus on the flaw. As a result, the woman agreed to undergo a difficult procedure to remove it. After the procedure, the birthmark faded and disappeared, but the woman began to fade as well, and died shortly thereafter. The birthmark was connected to the mystery of her life and beauty. It was the bond by which an angelic spirit kept itself housed in a mortal human body. But that wasn't enough for the husband. He wasn't satisfied with beauty of body and spirit. He wanted perfection, and as a result he ended up with nothing.

Marriages today tend to be founded on romantic love. We feel swept away by feelings of rapture. As one writer puts it, "You look for a person who throws you into a trance, and hope that when you come out of the trance, he turns out to be someone you can like." We say to ourselves, "I can't believe that someone that nice, someone that perfect actually loves me." We say to ourselves, "He/she makes me feel so good about myself," without realizing that when we say that, we are admitting that we don't really love the other person. We are using the other person to help us love ourselves. "If someone that nice loves me, I must be truly lovable."

But if romantic attraction is the basis for love among courting couples, it is no long-term basis on which to build a marriage. The illusion of perfection in the other will not last. And that is why *the essence of marital love is not romance but forgiveness.*

Let me be very clear as to what I mean by that. To define love as forgiveness does not mean that a man can inform his wife about his extramarital affairs and when she becomes upset, say, "The fact that she can't forgive me proves that she doesn't love me and that justifies my doing what I did." Defining love as forgiveness does not require a battered wife to continue to suffer physical abuse at the hands of an abusive husband. Neither does it require you to let yourself be exploited and walked over without a protest. Forgiveness as the truest form of love means accepting without bitterness the flaws and imperfections of our partner, and praying that our partner accepts our flaws as well. Romantic love *overlooks* faults ("love is blind") in an effort to persuade ourselves that we deserve a perfect partner. Mature marital love sees faults clearly and forgives them, understanding that there are no perfect people, that we don't have to pretend perfection, and that an imperfect spouse is all that an imperfect person like us can aspire to. ("For years, I was looking for the perfect man, and when I finally found him, it turned out he was looking for the perfect woman and that wasn't me.")

My wife and I spend ten days every winter at a fitness resort in Tucson, Arizona. We hike and exercise all day, and usually attend the lectures on healthier lifestyles in the evening. One evening, the topic of the lecture was "Communication Problems Between Men and Women," based on the bestselling book *Men Are from Mars, Women Are from Venus.* The tension in the room was palpable, very different from the mood when the lecture topic was exercise or low-fat diets. You sensed it in the nervous jokes and comments people made.

One woman told the story of how she and

her husband had spent an extra hour driving to a gathering, arriving embarrassingly late, because her husband stubbornly refused to stop and ask directions. The other women in the room laughed knowingly, the men nodded in embarrassed recognition. But one attractive young woman got up and said, "If some man did that to me, I'd get out of the car, take a cab home, and never speak to him again." I was tempted to ask her (but didn't), "Have you no faults of your own that you would expect someone who loved you to tolerate? Have you no exasperating quirks that could drive a person crazy if they didn't love you enough to take you as you were?" I found myself wondering if that young woman (who, I noticed, was not wearing a wedding ring) might be a relative of the "season ticket lady" in Boston. An inability to love another person often expresses itself as an inability to forgive them for their all-too-human flaws. "I'm so good I don't have to put up with a flawed person like you."

I contrasted that young woman's remark with comments I had read by a woman married to a man who was slightly manic-depressive. She never knew when her husband would be rational, when he would be depressed for no reason, and when he would, in his manic phase, have to be talked out of some unrealistic idea. Friends asked her why she stayed with him when he made life so difficult for her, and she answered, "I've fallen in love with his core." While she did not enjoy some of the specific things he did, she loved the total person behind the actions and chose to "buy the package." In her therapist's words, "though her husband's behavior would probably never change, she could acknowledge and accept his imperfections and still love his core."

The embarrassing secret is that many of us are reluctant to forgive. We nurture grievances because that makes us feel morally superior. Withholding forgiveness gives us a sense of power, often power over someone who otherwise leaves us feeling powerless. The only power we have over them is the power to remain angry at them. At some level, we enjoy the role of being the long-suffering, aggrieved party. The Book of Deuteronomy in the Bible makes a distinction between murder, which is to be punished severely, and accidental manslaughter, which is treated more leniently. But how do we know if a fatal injury was caused deliberately or accidentally? Deuteronomy says (Deut. 4:42) if the person who caused the injury had not been feuding with the victim over the previous two or three days, we can assume it was an accident.

Commenting on that verse, the sages of the Talmud offer a fascinating psychological insight. They say that the normal life span of a quarrel is two or three days. If a person hurts or offends you, you are entitled to be upset with him for that long. (We are talking about routine arguments and misunderstandings here, not major offenses.) If the bitter feelings extend into a fourth day, it is because you are choosing to hold on to them. You are nursing the grievance, keeping it on artificial life support, instead of letting it die a natural death.

There may be a certain emotional satisfaction in claiming the role of victim, but it is a bad idea for two reasons. First, it estranges you from a person you could be close to. (And if it becomes a habit, as it all too often does, it estranges you from many people you could be close to.) And secondly, it accustoms you to seeing yourself in the role of victim — helpless, passive, preyed upon by others. Is that shallow feeling of moral superiority worth learning to see yourself that way?

Pastoral counselor David Norris puts it this way: "Forgiveness involves a letting go not only of the negative energy connecting with an injury, but also of the meanings which we learned as a result of that and similar injuries throughout one's life." By "negative energy," Norris means the sense of bitterness and resentment we carry with us when we remember how someone has hurt us. When I would counsel a divorcée still seething about her husband's having left her for another woman years ago and having fallen behind on child support payments, and she would ask me, "How can you expect me to forgive him after what he's done to me and the children?" I would answer, "I'm not asking you to forgive him because what he did wasn't so terrible; it *was* terrible. I'm suggesting that you forgive him because he doesn't deserve to have this power to turn you into a bitter, resentful woman. When he left, he gave up the right to inhabit your life and mind to the degree that you're letting him. Your being angry at him doesn't harm him, but it hurts you. It's turning you into someone you don't really want to be. Release that anger, not for his sake — he probably doesn't deserve it — but for your sake, so that the real you can reemerge." And when the negative energy distances us from someone we want to be connected with — a husband or wife, a brother or sister, a close friend who has disappointed us — it is that much more important that we learn to discharge it.

By "the meanings which we learned," Norris refers to the sense of unworthiness we feel about ourselves when someone we care about has mistreated us or let us down. These offenses bother us so deeply not only because they are wrong in and of themselves, but because they hit us where we are most vulnerable. They touch our fear that we may really not be lovable people after all. The longer we nurse a grievance, saying to ourselves, "That person doesn't care about my feelings," the more we replay the message in our minds "My feelings must not be worth caring about." When we forgive, when we come to see what someone did to us not as the result of malice or the dismissal of our feelings, but as the result of human weakness, impatience, and imperfection, we not only free the other person from the role of villain; we free ourselves from the role of victim.

Boston Globe columnist Linda Weltner makes the point in a story she tells. She remembers sitting in a park watching children at play. Two children get into an argument, and one says to the other, "I hate you! I'm never going to play with you again!" For a few minutes, they play separately, and then they are back sharing their toys with each other. Ms. Weltner remarks to another mother, "How do children do that? How do they manage to be so angry with each other one minute, and the best of friends the next?" The other mother answers, "It's easy. They choose happiness over righteousness."

We too have the power to choose happiness over righteousness. Righteousness means remembering every time someone hurt us or disappointed us, and never letting them forget it (and — frightening thought — giving them the right to remember every time we hurt them or let them down and constantly remind us of it). Happiness means giving people the right to be human, to be weak and selfish and occasionally forgetful, and realizing that we have no alternative to living with imperfect people. (I once saw a button that read, "Never attribute to malice what can be explained by stupidity." I might emend that to read, "Never attribute to malice what can be explained by human frailty and imperfection.")

The quest for righteousness estranges people from each other; the quest for happiness enables them to get past their shortcomings and connect with each other. And strange as it may seem, happiness may be a more authentically religious value than righteousness.

Winter Light is one of the Swedish movie director Ingmar Bergman's less-known films, but for some reason — maybe because its hero is a clergyman, maybe because I could understand it better than most of his other films — it has always been one of my favorites. It takes place in a small seacoast village in Sweden during the winter. The world outside is cold and bleak. The hours of sunlight are brief and the sources of warmth are few. The central characters are a Lutheran minister, Pastor Thomas Ericson, and his girlfriend, Marta, a local schoolteacher. The pastor is still grieving for the loss of his wife to cancer four years earlier, and it has turned him into a bitter, joyless man, as reflected in the cold, austere feelings of his service, scarcely warmer than the weather outside. Ericson is angry at God for letting his wife die. When a depressed congregant hesitantly approaches him to ask about reasons for going on living, the pastor rambles on about his own disappointments in life and blurts out, "God is a monster!" The congregant commits suicide shortly afterward, leaving a wife and young family.

As we get to know Thomas and Marta better, we come to realize that although Marta repeatedly claims that she is not religious, was raised without faith, and does not believe in prayer, she is the most religious character in the picture because she is able to forgive and to love. She continues to love Thomas, though he mistreats her cruelly. She understands that his disappointment with himself and his life expresses itself in anger toward God and toward her. She admits that once God answered her prayer. She had asked God what to do with her life, and God led her to understand that at the core of her soul was the desire to live for someone. Marta can love Thomas despite his conspicuous faults; he cannot love her in return, because like the husband in the Hawthorne story, her flaws blind him to her redeeming qualities.

In a key scene in the movie, Marta remembers how one evening she was suffering terribly from eczema, causing her hands to rub raw and bleed and spreading to her feet and scalp. (The symbolism, paralleling the stigmata of Jesus on the cross, identifies Marta, despite her protestations of not being religious, as a Christ figure, the one who lives for others, the one who loves us despite our flaws. When we first meet her, she is bringing hot coffee to people in a cold office.) She turned to Thomas, her minister and her lover, for a sign of compassion, but he was so revolted by her wounds that he could not even pray for her. He could not love an imperfect Marta. Later in the film, he declares that he is disgusted by her nearsightedness, her queasy stomach, her monthly periods, even as he is annoyed by the concerns and imperfections of his congregants. Thomas's religion is a mockery of true religion, because it condemns people for being flawed and imperfect instead of reaching out to them in love to bind their wounds. In one scene which I have never permitted myself as a clergyman to forget, the couple meets a young boy returning from school. Thomas scolds him for not enrolling in the church's confirmation class. Marta asks him, "How is your brother? I heard that he was ill." We leave the movie having learned the lesson that if we cannot love imperfect people, if we cannot forgive them for their exasperating faults, we will condemn ourselves to a life of loneliness, because imperfect people are the only kind we will ever find. Winter light may be pale and unreliable, but when the world turns cold, it may be the only light and warmth we have.

If we are lucky, marriage means finding the person who makes us whole, as Adam and Eve were reunited to form a single being. It means finding the husband who will encourage our masculine side to emerge, or the wife who will help us give birth to the feminine side buried within us. If we are lucky, marriage means finding someone to tell us that the way we are is just fine, and there is nothing we need to change (which, by the way, will make it easier for us to change).

When I look back on my thirty years as a congregational rabbi, and all the married couples who came to see me with their problems, I recall one pattern of disagreement that repeated itself so often and with such similarity that I sometimes felt I was watching different actors auditioning from the same script. Something that had once been a source of attraction had become a cause of conflict.

"I fell in love with him because he was so lively and outgoing, while I had always been so shy and timid. Now I hate it when he makes a fool of himself at social gatherings."

"I thought her relaxed attitude about time would cure me of my compulsiveness, and for a while it did. But now we fight all the time about my having to wait for her, and about our almost missing planes and coming late to movies because she's never ready."

"I was drawn to him because of his ambition to get ahead and make something of himself, something my father and brother never had. I didn't know then that it would mean my staying home alone at night while he worked late at the office."

"I thought it was great that she was so careful with money when we were dating and engaged, because I was a guy who spent it as fast as I made it. But now it drives me crazy. Every time we need to buy something, we get into an argument because she wants to buy the cheapest model available even if it's a piece of junk we'll have to replace in a year."

We are attracted to people who seem to have what we lack, and who therefore promise to make us whole. When it works, it is wonderful, Adam and Eve restored to the unity that prevailed in Eden. In the words of Genesis, psychologically as well as sexually we "become one flesh." But two people with complementary personalities don't always fit together as neatly as pieces of a jigsaw puzzle. Sometimes there are mismatched edges that have to be worn down with love and patience. And that is why forgiveness, the readiness to accept traits in our partner that would drive us crazy if we didn't love them, and to accept them without a sense of martyrdom, sacrifice, or keeping score ("I put up with your snoring; how dare you criticize me for messing up the checkbook?") is the essence of married love.

John Milton's seventeenth century epic poem *Paradise Lost* is the classic treatment of the Garden of Eden story in English literature. I confess it is not one of my favorite books. The overblown language and smug theology are not to my taste, and I am embarrassed by the frequent reminders that the role of woman is to serve man and that man sins by taking woman's words too seriously. (I am reminded as I write this of a test in a humanities class in my freshman year at college. It consisted of two questions: (1) Of all the books we have read this year, which one did you enjoy least? (2) To what limitation in yourself would you attribute this inability to appreciate an acknowledged classic?)

But there is one dimension of the poem I do appreciate. Amidst all of its mistrust of women, it says something very thoughtful about the marital relationship. When we first meet Adam and Eve, they are holding hands.

In fact, they never let go of each other's hand, as if they were a single being, a single soul, in two bodies. But then at one point Eve (whom Milton repeatedly blames for the foolishness that leads to the Fall) suggests that she and Adam work separately to get more work done in less time. This attitude of self-sufficiency, "I'm fine by myself, I don't need anyone else," leaves her vulnerable to temptation and sin. She eats the forbidden fruit and gives some to Adam. Their love, which had been pure and innocent, is now contaminated by selfishness and lust. They are now separate beings, no longer holding hands, each one looking to satisfy his or her own needs without regard for the other. They are to be expelled from Paradise. Indeed, one has the impression that they have already lost Paradise spiritually even before they lose it geographically. But then, on the last page of the poem, Eve speaks of her regret for what she has caused, offers the hope that they can still find happiness in this strife-torn world, and holds out her hand to Adam. The poem concludes with these lines:

The world was all before them . . .
They *hand in hand* with wandering steps
     and slow
Through Eden took their solitary way.

I believe that husbands and wives have the right, indeed have the need, to be separate people. They don't have to like the same foods, enjoy the same friends, have the same hobbies. It is not a betrayal of your spouse to respond differently to a business failure or the death of a child. We misunderstand Milton, and we misunderstand marriage, if we take his symbolism literally and think that we are committing a sin by wanting to do something by ourselves without bringing our husband or wife along. Milton is saying something very different when he describes Adam and Eve as holding hands, dropping hands, and then reaching out to each other again. He is saying that true love and marriage offer us something that we can find nowhere else in life, the opportunity to transcend our separateness by merging with another person.

There are lots of places in today's world where we can get our individual needs met — a good meal, a comfortable bed, even sexual release. But only in the permanence of marriage can we meet our existential human need to transcend the loneliness of being an individual, to find the person who makes us whole, who provides us with what we lack and liberates the qualities hidden within us, and join with that person to "become one flesh." And we can only do that the way Adam and Eve do it on the very last page of Milton's tragic poem, two fallen people getting over their anger and disappointment with each other, reaching out to take each other's hand and together search for warmth and love in a cold and daunting world.

But when a man and a woman learn to love each other with the love that sees and forgives faults, they can do more than escape their loneliness. The Jewish mystics believed that what happens on earth reflects what is happening in heaven, and vice versa. Heaven is affected by our earthly behavior. In one astonishing statement, they say, "The world is unredeemed because God's masculine side is separated from God's feminine side, and when husband and wife come together in love, they restore God's unity and bring the Redemption closer." If a young person's love is selfish, concerned with validating our own sense of worth and meeting our own needs, and if mature love is mutual, letting the boundaries of self blur as we become one with another person, feeling that person's pain and pleasure as if they were our own, the mystics are telling us that there is yet a higher form of love, a love that redeems the world from brokenness.

It is such a brave thing to truly love another person, but it is such a necessary thing, for our own sake, for the other person's sake, and for the world's sake. Men and women are so different from each other — different needs, different expectations, different ways of communicating. They are like fire and water. How can we hope for them to get along with each other, let alone make each other whole? Interestingly, there is an old Jewish legend that when God created the heaven and the earth, heaven was made up of fire (the sun) and water (the rainclouds). The sun said, "If I wanted to, I could evaporate those clouds and rule in heaven all by myself. But without rain, the world could not exist." The clouds said, "If we had a mind to, we could extinguish that sun and have heaven to ourselves. But without the sun, how would the world survive?" So they each decided to sacrifice their ambition, to restrain their powers, and make room for each other in heaven. By learning to live with their opposites, they made heaven complete and made the world safe.

What does it mean to say that God's masculine side is separated from God's feminine side? I take it to mean that when men and women are angry at each other, when they are resentful and suspicious, God is less present in the world. When we are in love, the world looks different. We feel the presence of God in the gift of being able to love. When we are hurt, when we are disappointed, that takes the glow from the world. I am prepared to believe that, when so many marriages all over the world have sunk into sullenness and resentment, when so many people stand outside their marriages evaluating them and wondering if they would be happier somewhere else, that pollutes the air. It makes the world a sullen, suspicious place in which we learn to mistrust other people and be on guard at all times. If all those unhappy couples could recapture the sense they once had of being in love, a feeling which enabled them to enjoy both the sunshine and the rain, if they could overcome their disappointments with each other, disappointments based on unrealistic expectations, and choose happiness over righteousness, they would have the power to cleanse the air, to redeem the world and bring the presence of God back into it, a God who loves us enough to forgive our faults. When we re-pair ourselves, when we rediscover the fulfillment of being a pair, two souls combining to form a single complete being, we can repair the world.

Chapter 6

CAIN AND ABEL
Is There Enough Love to Go Around?

Some people understand the theological construct known as Original Sin to mean that, as descendants of Adam and Eve, we inherit from them the stain of having disobeyed and offended God, either like children inheriting a genetic defect passed on to them by their parents or like children having to assume the obligations of a debt left by parents. Others, identifying sin with sexual lust, understand it to mean that each of us is born a sinner because each of us was born as the result of a sexual, therefore sinful, act. This interpretation is strengthened by the Christian teaching that Jesus was born of a virgin, without requiring a sexual act. Still others, following the more sophisticated interpretation of Protestant theologian Reinhold Niebuhr, understand Original Sin to mean that, because human life is so morally complex, every human being will inevitably do something, probably many things, against the will of God. Even the person who is always righteous will find it difficult to resist the swell of pride as he contemplates his righteousness.

But whatever their interpretations, all of them trace the notion of Original Sin back to Adam and Eve and the fruit of the forbidden tree. They would probably be surprised to learn that the Book of Genesis, and in fact the entire Hebrew Bible, never refers to that incident as a sin. The first time the word "sin" appears in the Bible, it refers not to Adam and Eve but to Cain and Abel.

Their story is as familiar to us as that of their parents. When Adam and Eve were exiled from Eden, they no longer had access to the Tree of Life. Instead of being immortal themselves, they began to have children, with the prospect of living on vicariously through their offspring. They had two sons, Cain and Abel. Cain grew up to be a farmer, while Abel was a shepherd. One day, each brought an offering to God, Cain from the first fruits of the soil and Abel from the firstborn of his flocks. For whatever reason, God accepted Abel's offering but rejected Cain's. Cain grew murderously jealous. God warned him, "Why are you distressed? If you do right, you will be uplifted. But if you do not do right, *sin crouches at the door,* its urge toward you, but you can be its master" (Genesis 4:6–7). Unheeding, Cain went on to kill his brother and then responded to God's query "Where is your brother?" by answering, "I don't know; am I my brother's keeper?" Cain's punishment for having polluted the soil by spilling innocent blood on it was that he was to be an eternal wanderer, forbidden to have a piece of earth to call his own.

Some scholars see the story of Cain and Abel as representing an ancient conflict between the shepherds who wanted their flocks to be able to roam free, and the farmers who tried to fence off a piece of land and prevent the sheep from grazing there (as in a hundred western movies I have seen). The nomadic shepherds thought that farmers were wicked people for trying to claim some of God's earth as their private domain, and then violating Mother Earth with their sharp iron plows and tools instead of waiting for it to yield its bounty as shepherds did.

But, anthropological scholarship aside, most of us reading the story recognize it for what it is, the all-too-familiar feeling of one sibling toward another, "I hate you, I wish you were dead, because Daddy and Mommy love you more than they love me." It would seem that children, so dependent on their parents' love, find it hard to be angry at their parents for playing favorites, and easier to be angry at their brother or sister for being favored. And if God is the Superparent, it must have been devastating for Cain to have God prefer Abel's offering to his. Several years ago, playwright Peter Shaffer fastened on the obscure fact that Mozart's middle name was Amadeus, meaning "beloved by God," and wrote a play about the murderous jealousy felt by one of Mozart's contemporaries as he contemplated the fact that God had blessed Mozart with so much more genius than He had bestowed on any of His other children.

In fact, to an astonishing degree, the Book of Genesis is a book about sibling rivalry carried to extremes. A few pages after Cain kills Abel, Isaac and Ishmael, the two sons of Abraham by different wives, are bitter rivals, resulting in Ishmael's banishment and near death. Isaac goes on to have twin sons, Jacob and Esau. Jacob cheats Esau out of the paternal blessing, prompting Esau to vow to kill him. Several of Jacob's sons assault the favored brother, Joseph, nearly kill him, and sell him into slavery. How many children, reading those Bible tales of the rage of the displaced older child, the jealousy of the younger child, and the vulnerability of the favored child, felt that they were reading the story of their own lives in the pages of the Bible? And isn't that why those ancient tales have the power over us that they do?

It is important to notice that in the biblical story, God warns Cain of the danger of sin *before* he murders his brother. Before Cain is guilty of murder, he is guilty of the sin of hatred and resentment. The story of Cain and Abel is not about the conflict between farmers and shepherds. It is about the pain and anger we all feel when we suspect that someone else is loved more than we are. Older siblings resent being displaced by the new baby who is fussed over while they are ignored. Younger siblings resent being told that they can't share in what their older brothers and sisters are doing. Bright children feel hurt when their siblings are celebrated for their looks or athletic gifts, and those other siblings feel put down when the bright one in the family is honored for an outstanding report card. Even when parents don't actually play favorites, we perceive favoritism every time one of the others is praised or paid attention to and we are not (even if the attention is for illness or misbehavior, and even if we were the one fussed over an hour earlier).

As I read the biblical narrative, the Original Sin is not disobedience nor is it lust. The Original Sin that affects virtually every one of us and leads to other, worse sins is *the belief that there is not enough love to go around,* and therefore when someone else is loved, he or she is stealing that love from us. Later in Genesis, when Jacob disguises himself as his older brother Esau and obtains by trickery the blessing meant for the firstborn, Esau plaintively responds, "Have you but one blessing, father? Bless me also" (Gen. 27:38). Our primal fear is that our parents don't have enough love for us all, and someone else may be getting part of our share. Later in life, when we are passed over for a promotion, when our doctor or our clergyman gets our name wrong, when someone pushes ahead of us on line, we may respond with a disproportionate sense of hurt because the experience reawakens childhood feelings that our parents may love someone else more than they love us. (Might this be why infidelity has greater power to destroy a marriage than physical abuse, alcoholism, gambling, or criminal activity?)

There is a line in John Steinbeck's novel *East of Eden* that captures that feeling. "The greatest terror a child can have is that he is not loved, and rejection is the hell he fears."

Steinbeck's novel is in fact a retelling of the story of Cain and Abel, with overtones of the Garden of Eden story as well. At one point, the author puts these words (and, I suspect, his own feelings) into the mouth of one of his characters: "Two stories have haunted us and followed us from our beginnings. We carry them with us like invisible tails — the story of original sin and the story of Cain and Abel. I don't understand either of them. I don't understand either of them at all, but I feel them."

East of Eden is built around two sets of brothers, each carrying the initials C and A, Charles and Adam Trask and Adam's sons, Cal and Aron. In each case, the brothers are opposite personalities, one cynical and hardened by life, the other soft and innocent. Steinbeck does a superb job of making Cal Trask, the "Cain" of the book, a sympathetic figure (as did James Dean in the movie version) so that we feel the unfairness of his being rejected when he brings his father the hard-earned first fruits of his farming labors. Cal has tried so hard to be a good son, believing that he can win his father's love that way. He doesn't realize that his father's favoring Aron has less to do with Cal's behavior and more to do with the emotional scars Adam Trask carries from his own boyhood and unhappy marriage, painful memories that Cal unintentionally evokes.

In generation after generation, the Bible presents us with a mismatched set of brothers or sisters, each person with qualities his or her sibling doesn't have, each pair destined to come into conflict with each other because they are so opposite, not realizing that if they could come together, they would make one whole person: the evil Cain and the innocent victim Abel; the wild Ishmael and the obedient Isaac; the boorish Esau and the mother-pleasing Jacob, the beautiful but barren Rachel and her plain sister Leah with a houseful of children — almost as if siblings divided the available personality traits between them: "You take these and I'll take the others."

In the fall of 1992, just about the time that Americans were electing Bill Clinton president, an article appeared in a Boston newspaper noting how many recent American presidents had younger brothers who embarrassed them. President Clinton has his recovering-drug-addict stepbrother, Roger. One remembers Jimmy Carter and Billy Carter, Lyndon Johnson and his black-sheep brother, Sam Houston Johnson. Richard Nixon's younger brother periodically would try to cash in on the family name. Senator Edward Kennedy, youngest of the Kennedy brothers, did things when he was young and when he was older that embarrassed his family.

The article went on to suggest that parents often mold children from infancy to fill certain family roles. In a common scenario, the eldest child will be raised to be the responsible one, the one who will carry the family banner, be the good boy or girl in school and elsewhere, and go on to success that will make the parents proud. A disproportionate number of presidents, senators, jet pilots, Rhodes scholars, and CEOs of corporations have been firstborn sons (as were Newton, Einstein, Freud, Julius Caesar, and Winston Churchill). If firstborns are attracted to positions of authority, later-borns tend to grow up to challenge authority. (Copernicus and Darwin were younger brothers.) These firstborn children are often raised to be serious and goal-oriented. The child who comes along later, by an unconscious division of labor, is permitted all the qualities denied to the firstborn. He can be irresponsible and parents will see him as fun-loving. He will be encouraged to have more modest ambitions, and his bringing home a mediocre report card will not be nearly as upsetting as it would be if his older sibling did it. (Think of all those Grimm's fairy tales where the eldest brother inherits the farm, the second son goes off to join the army, and the youngest, often referred to as a "simpleton," is left to "seek his fortune," that is, to fend for himself. Or the parable of the Prodigal Son in the New Testament (Luke 15:11–32), where it is the younger brother who leaves home and wastes his inheritance. It is fascinating to remember that John F. Kennedy was a *younger* brother when he was growing up, with tacit permission to be carefree and slightly irresponsible. Only after his older brother's death was he propelled into a position of striving for fame and success. Could it be that some of the less flattering things we have learned about JFK's private life resulted from this tension of not knowing if he was the responsible eldest brother or the carefree younger one?)

One of the oldest photographs in our family album shows me (at about age four) standing between my two-year-old brother and a small cat. It is clear that we are both afraid of the cat, but as the older one, I already felt a sense of responsibility to put myself between my brother and the cat. I have often thought that there was something defining about that photograph. During our years of growing up together, I am sure there were times when my brother would have liked to be the one in charge and I would have loved to have him step in and relieve me of that responsibility (and from time to time, he did). There must have been times when I resented my parents for always expecting me to be the model of goodness. I might have enjoyed being permitted occasional moments of irresponsibility. As one firstborn wrote in a memoir, "Early on, I was pushed into an 'oldness' that I wasn't ready for. My younger sister looked at my position in the family with envy because she saw me as the more privileged one who was allowed to be grown up when she wasn't. Well, I'd gladly give up being everyone's big sister." For the most part, I was raised to be the older brother and my brother to be the younger. I was two years old when he was born, and he could never catch up. I would go to school before he did, go to college, get married, get a job before he did, not because I was more able but simply because, through no merit of my own, I had been born first. But it defined me as the trailblazer. Much of the story of my life has been a story of my willingly taking charge, taking on responsibility, often to the point of leaving others to say, "He did it well and we appreciate it, but why did he have to do so much of it himself and leave so little for us to do except admire and thank him for it?" Much of the answer, I suspect, has to do with my being raised as a firstborn son.

Why do parents slot children into patterns of behavior from birth? Sometimes they are repeating patterns of their childhood ("he's a good-for-nothing just like my younger brother Alex. He even looks like Alex") or their cultural background ("girls don't need good grades; girls need to be popular"). Sometimes they are responding to the personalities of the infants themselves. I believe babies are born with personalities; some are more shy and some more outgoing from birth. Sometimes parents change from one baby to the next. Even full brothers and sisters don't really have the same mother and father, in the sense that the parents may have been insecure and inexperienced with the first child (maybe even resentful if it was an unplanned pregnancy) and more comfortable with later ones, or may have been totally available to the first child and have their time and strength divided by the time there are two or more. Sometimes when younger children choose not to compete with an older one who had a head start, and go off in another direction on their own, the parents affirm and encourage that choice. And very commonly, parents designate children to live out their own unfulfilled dreams and invest their egos in the child most likely to do that. I think of Isaac in the Bible favoring Esau for being the physically imposing man he never was, or all the fathers who were unsuccessful athletes and relate to the most athletically gifted of their sons differently than they do to their daughters or intellectually able boys.

The sibling conflicts in biblical stories foreshadow a pattern I have seen so often in troubled families. Even as the ancient Israelites would designate an animal as the scapegoat and symbolically unload all their sins on it before dispatching it to die in the wilderness, troubled families often designate one of their children to be "the bad one," to be manipulated in subtle ways to act out all the parts of the family dynamic that they are ashamed of, so that they can go to the school authorities or to the therapist and say, "Our other children are fine, but we just don't know what to do about Michael." This pattern is almost never imposed deliberately, but it is destructive to everyone involved, to the designated scapegoat most painfully, to his parents, who paint themselves into a corner of not being able to love one of their children, and to the designated "good" son or daughter as well.

The "bad" child feels guilty for the grief he is causing his parents, and will be somewhat bewildered at finding himself in that position. It is not something he remembers choosing. But the "good" child will often feel guilty at inheriting the role of the loved, praised child while seeing her brother be the object of verbal and physical punishment. More than that, the "good" child will often resent having to play the "good" role full-time even as her "problem" brother resents being cast as the troublemaker. She might much rather be a normal child than a model one, with good days and bad days, good report cards and bad report cards, but that is denied her. Children whose parents have suffered greatly (survivors of the Holocaust, parents burdened with health or financial problems) feel they have to "make it up to them" by being as perfect as possible. They have to inhibit their normal behavior to spare their parents further pain. (Did Cain become a tiller of the soil to replace the Garden his parents had been exiled from before he was born?) And if one child is seriously misbehaving, he will likely monopolize that role fully and leave his brothers and sisters to be the "good" ones ("I'm glad *you* don't cause me any problems"). They will have to swallow their resentment ("You pay more attention to him for being bad than you pay to me for being good") and repress a normal part of their personality (often to have it emerge as rebelliousness in their thirties or forties instead of in their teenage years, or as anger toward a dependent parent years later). In Sue Miller's novel *Family Pictures*, the heroine remembers her mother loving her autistic older brother no matter how out-of-bounds his behavior might be, but giving her the message that she would love her only if she were good, quiet, obedient, and happy, "my perfect baby." Faber and Mazlish, authors of *Siblings Without Rivalry*, offer a real-life parallel, quoting one woman saying to her mother, "Every time I tried to rebel, like when I cut school once in the fifth grade or when I refused to play the piano for company, all I ever heard was 'That's not like you, dear.' Do you know what it would have meant to me if just once you had said, 'You don't have to be so good all the time. You don't have to be so perfect. You don't have to be mother's pleasure. You can be nasty, bratty, sloppy, *normal*, . . . and I'll love you just as much.' "

When a child has died, the surviving siblings often find themselves burdened by feelings of irrational, undeserved guilt and a self-imposed pressure to "make it up" to their parents by being a perfect replacement, living out the dead child's life in addition to their own, a pledge they are never able satisfactorily to fulfill. It may be a sense (usually unjustified) that they could have done something to prevent the death, or that their jealous, angry wishes might have caused it. It may be a form of survivior-guilt over being the one who survived, especially if the parents in their bereavement talk at length about the wonderful qualities of the child who died. The surviving siblings may say to themselves, "They wouldn't be nearly as broken up if I were the one who died and he were still alive." As many readers of this book know, my wife and I suffered the loss of a fourteen-year-old son. A few years later, I wrote a book out of that experience, *When Bad Things Happen to Good People*. Just as our daughter was beginning to come to terms with her brother's death and get used to having us to herself, she had to cope with her father running around the country appearing on television to talk about her dead brother instead of being there to help her with her homework. *People* magazine added to the problem by running an article about my book which featured a picture of our son, Aaron, and the caption "Four years after his death, he is still the most important member of the family."

Even a brother or sister whom we never knew can be a source of guilt feelings. Francine Klagsbrun interrupts her psychological study of sibling relationships, *Mixed Feelings*, to remember that her parents had an older child who died before she was born, and reflects, "Would my parents have stopped at two if Sidney had lived? Did we swap lives, he and I, he losing his so that I could be born?"

It is interesting that so much has been written about the Oedipus complex, the conflict between father and son, and on the repressed incestuous feelings of fathers and daughters, mothers and sons, for each other. But so little has been written about the problems brothers and sisters have with each other. Francine Klagsbrun writes, "We are accustomed to analyzing (often incessantly) our relationships with parents. But when people try to analyze their attachments to their brothers and sisters, they may find themselves tripping over words. . . . I would argue, in fact, that sibling memories can sometimes have an even greater impact on our adult relationships than parental ones. Because so many of our interactions are with peers — with our spouses, friends, or co-workers — it is easier in many cases to identify them as sibling substitutes than as parent stand-ins, and to direct toward them many of the attitudes and feelings we had toward brothers and sisters." Is it possible that our sense of who we are is shaped by our parents and our spouse, but our habits of relating to other people tend to reflect how we related to our brothers and sisters?

Is there a cure for this Original Sin, the fear of siblings that they will go unloved if their parents have someone else to lavish their love on? There may very well be. Coming to terms with our feelings of sibling jealousy may in fact be an important part of growing up. Klagsbrun, based on a hypothesis of Sigmund Freud, writes, "Once children recognize that they cannot win through rivalry and that they must share their parents' love with their siblings, they begin to identify with other children like themselves. Through that identification come the seeds of a sense of justice, a decision that if we cannot be loved more than another, all must be treated equally and fairly."

In other words, the story does not have

to end with Cain killing Abel in an effort to be the sole recipient of God's, or Eve's, love. (There is an ancient legend, written thousands of years before Freud, that Cain and Abel were quarreling over which one would become Eve's mate after Adam died.) The story could describe Cain and Abel realizing how much they have in common by being dependent on the whims of an arbitrary God, and working together to try to understand and please Him. After all, brothers and sisters don't only fight. They share more, over more years and often more intimately, than they do with parents or even spouses. (I have lived many more years, and much more closely, with my wife than I ever lived at home with my brother, and shared much more with her. But it will still happen that a code word from a childhood game will cause my brother and me to dissolve into helpless laughter, leaving my wife baffled and uncomprehending.) Once the rivalry is put in perspective, once the Original Sin of feeling that another person's love was stolen from you is perceived for the error it is, there is a lot to build on.

If the Book of Genesis is a chronicle of sibling rivalry, it is also a book of sibling reconciliation. Isaac and Ishmael come together at the grave of their father, Abraham.

Jacob and Esau overcome their memories of past hurts and fears, and fall into each other's arms after twenty years of estrangement. And in the greatest story ever written about brothers overcoming hatred and jealousy, Joseph is reunited with the brothers who sold him into slavery. For years, Joseph dreamed of getting even with them (and perhaps getting even with his father for making him the favored son and the object of his brothers' hatred). But when he finally had the power to do so, when he was a high government official and they were famine-ridden shepherds begging for food, Joseph discovered that he didn't really want revenge. He wanted family. And he couldn't have family unless both sides transcended the hatreds and hurt feelings of their growing-up years.

I know so many people who have condemned themselves to a life of estrangement, who insist on leaving empty places at every wedding, birthday party, and family gathering because years ago, they had a quarrel with a brother or sister based on the Original Sin of believing that there wasn't enough love for everyone, and if someone took more than his share, there wouldn't be any left for them. Decades had passed, parents had grown old and might have died, but they still argued about which of them their mother had loved more when they were children. Maybe they had parents who weren't very good at knowing how to love several children at the same time. (As Faber and Mazlish point out, children don't really want to be loved *equally*. They want to be loved *uniquely*, for their own special selves, and not every parent knows how to do that.) Maybe they were raised by manipulative parents who made them compete to be loved best. But years later, their every encounter is contaminated by the guilt of being favored or the hurt of being overlooked. Both sides carry around mental images of each other that are decades old. They need to realize that just as they and their brothers and sisters no longer resemble the childhood photographs in the family album, they no longer resemble the mental stereotypes each is carrying around in his mind. When Jacob and Esau met after twenty years of separation, each found that his memory of his brother was twenty years out of date. Each had been hating or fearing a person who no longer existed, a person who had been replaced years ago by a more mature figure, tempered by experience and by life's hard lessons. Countless times, I have sat in the family room of a funeral chapel before a service as the children of the elderly parent who died assembled from their various directions. Sometimes when there had been a family feud (in maybe a third of all the families I dealt with!), the brothers and sisters made a point of sitting at opposite ends of the room and taking their turn speaking to me. But more often, they would reach out to each other, hesitantly at first, afraid of being rejected, but in that moment of confronting their shared memories and their shared sense of mortality, falling into each other's arms and saying, "Why did we have to wait this long? Why did it take this to get us into the same room together?" (I recently heard the true story of two brothers who had an argument and spent twenty years not speaking to each other. When one died, the other broke down and sobbed, "Now I don't have Sam not to talk to any more.")

Sometimes the gulf that separated brothers and sisters during their years of growing up can be narrowed later in life as they diminish the differences between them that loomed so large when they were small. Just as many men in middle age let their buried feminine side emerge, competing less and connecting more, and just as many women, at an equivalent age, give themselves permission to be assertive for themselves instead of living for and through others, many brothers and sisters reach for wholeness by outgrowing the roles they were assigned in childhood and "turning into each other." The entrepreneur takes early retirement to teach at a local community college, while his bookish brother begins to track his investments in the stock market. The career woman gives herself over totally to her new career as a mother, while her younger sister, married at nineteen and a mother at twenty, goes out and gets a job now that her children are teenagers. And if they are smart and lucky, each will give the other the benefit of their years of experience.

A friend of mine, a physician in Boston, shared this memory with me: "Ours was the classic story of the overachieving older brother and the underachieving younger one. I went to medical school; my brother dropped out of college and went to San Francisco to play the guitar on a street corner in Haight-Ashbury. My mother would boast about my grades, my appointments, my publications, and change the subject when people asked about Stanley. When my mother died, I came down from Boston for the funeral; Stan flew in from California. On the afternoon before the funeral service, I was sitting there with my mother's address book in my lap, calling all of her friends to tell them about the service, while my brother was stretched out on the couch, resting. I was getting tired of making the phone calls, and resenting the fact that I had to do all of it myself, as I had spent my whole life doing while my brother goofed off. I was on the verge of saying something harsh to him, but instead I somehow found myself saying, 'Stan, why don't you take this book and make the rest of the calls?' He said 'Sure,' got up from the couch, and did a really good job of it. I think he appreciated being asked to be useful. But I suspect that if I hadn't said something, we would have continued on those well-worn paths, me feeling put upon and responsible and Stan feeling shut out and rejected. All it took was a few words to change the pattern. Stan and I are a lot closer now than we were for years. We've found out we're a lot more alike than we ever thought. And I find myself wondering how our lives might have been different, had I spoken those words a few years earlier."

Some years ago, my wife and I were vacationing in Jerusalem. I was on my way to pray at the Western Wall, the surviving remnant of the ancient Temple, when I saw a crowd gathered around a street-corner preacher. I stopped to listen, and heard this story: In a small town in Poland, where most of the Jews were poor and unlearned, and where they had to compete against each other to eke out a living, there lived one man who was widely admired for his learning, his wealth, and his piety. One day, a dozen community leaders were pleased and astonished to receive an invitation to his home: "You are invited to Reb Isaac's home next Tuesday evening at six o'clock for a dinner worthy of Paradise." They could hardly wait for Tuesday to arrive. Dinner at Reb Isaac's! A meal worthy of Paradise! They all showed up promptly at six and were ushered into the dining room, where the table was elegantly set with dishes, glasses, and silver. When they were seated, a servant brought Reb Isaac a roll over which he recited the traditional blessing. The servant then set a bowl of soup before him, but none for the guests. Reb Isaac began to eat his soup, commenting, "Mmm, this is such good soup. I don't remember when I've had such tasty soup." The guests were puzzled; why weren't they being served as well? When Reb Isaac finished his soup, he motioned to his servant, who cleared the dish and returned a moment later with a plate of meat and vegetables for the host, and again nothing for the guests. Reb Isaac continued eating, saying, "Oh, this is so good. You have no idea what you're missing. This is so tasty, I love it." Finally one of the invited guests blurted out, "Reb Isaac, I don't understand. Have you brought us here to mock us? We were invited for a dinner worthy of Paradise, but you alone get the meal and we only get to watch you enjoy it. Why are you doing this to us?" Reb Isaac smiled. "A meal worthy of Paradise indeed. What did you think it would be? Is Paradise a famous restaurant? Is Paradise somewhere one wants to go for its fine food and wine? No, Paradise is a place where people love each other enough to take pleasure in another person's happiness. Paradise is any place where you can see your neighbor being successful and not envy him for it. Paradise is a place where people know that the truly important things in life are present in such abundance that there is plenty for everyone; we don't have to snatch them away from our neighbor. And now, if we have all learned that lesson, I'll have your dinner brought out to you."

Cain and Abel were the first human beings who had never lived in Paradise. They were the first human beings who had to compete for parental approval and contend with parental rejection. They never knew that a Paradise of their own making was within their reach. All they had to do was love each other enough to take pleasure in each other's success, instead of believing that the other's success came at their expense. All they had to do was understand that love is not like a bank account that is depleted as it is given away, where every dollar of love can only be spent once. Love is not like a buffet line where the person in front of you threatens to take too much and leave too little for you. Love is like a muscle; the more it is exercised today, the more it can be used tomorrow. Parents who love one child don't run out of love. They are practicing loving, and will be better at it when it comes to loving their other children. Whenever we "give away" our love, God replenishes it so that we become the channel of His love flowing to all of His children, a channel that never runs dry. Had Cain been wise enough to understand that, he might not have spent his days as a friendless wanderer. He might have reclaimed for himself and his descendants the Paradise that Adam and Eve had lost.

Chapter 7

LIFE AFTER EDEN

When God confronted Adam and Eve with the consequences of their having gained knowledge of Good and Evil, when He "condemned" them to being human, He specified three areas in which their lives would be more difficult, more pain-filled, than the lives of the animals they were leaving behind in the Garden. He told Adam that he would have to earn a living "by the sweat of (his) brow." Employment would be problematic and creativity would be painful. God told Eve that the two forms of loving that would be the twin pillars of her life, her sexual attachment to her husband and her parental involvement with her children, would be more complicated than the mating and breeding habits of other creatures. And He told them both that they would spend the rest of their days "in the valley of the shadow of death." All animals (except the simplest life forms) would die. But only human beings would live with the daily knowledge of their mortality.

Because we have been brought up to read the story of the Garden of Eden as an account of sin and punishment, we have read those verses as Adam's and Eve's punishments for their disobedience, a series of afflictions which we, their descendants, have inherited from them. So we have resented having to work and looked forward to retirement. We have lamented the fact that love is so elusive, that it is so difficult to find the right life partner, so painful to be rejected in love, and so frustrating to raise a child. And we have come to see death as the ultimate insult, the ultimate negation, putting every one of us at risk every day of having our lives cut short before we have been able to do all that we want to do. Life outside of Eden does seem to be somebody's idea of punishment, a blend of pain today and fear of tomorrow.

But throughout this book, I have been suggesting that our inheritance from Adam and Eve is not sin and punishment, but the burden and challenge of being truly human. Work, love, and the valley of the shadow may be painful, but how empty would our lives be, how much less human would our lives be, without them.

First, let me make the obvious point that not everything that is hard is bad; not everything that is unpleasant is bad. I once heard an educator say of the young people she worked with, "They refused to be bored, so they could not be educated." Some things are worth working hard to achieve. Some things mean more to us *because* we had to work hard to do them. They give us a feeling of competence and accomplishment. (What fun is there in doing an easy crossword puzzle?)

But is it really a punishment to have to work? Granted, many men and women dislike their jobs, and I suspect we all have days when we would love to sleep late and linger over breakfast instead of going to work. But it may be that we dislike our jobs precisely because there is a basic human need to create, to participate in reshaping the world, and we feel frustrated in a job that does not give us the scope and challenge to do that.

Work makes us feel useful. It shapes our days and gives us somewhere to go when we get up in the morning, and that is not to be minimized. After our son's death, the leaders of my congregation asked me if I wanted to take a sabbatical for the rest of the year, staying away from work so that I could come to terms with the loss. A wise friend told me that it would be a mistake.

"The worst thing for you right now," he said, "would be to wake up seven days a week with nothing to do but sit around feeling sorry for yourself. You need to have your days structured." A man I know owns a meatpacking plant in the midwest. His company's motto is "People don't make sausages; sausages make people." That is, the purpose of the company is not to manufacture a product. The purpose is to give the people who work there the sense that they are competent, valued men and women. The meat products are by-products. He tells me proudly that his plant is more productive and has less absenteeism than its competitors.

Work lets us feel needed. I think of all the businessmen I know who say, "There are two reasons why I never take a vacation. First, I'm afraid the office won't be able to function without me. And second, I'm afraid it will." Why after all do so many lottery winners choose to continue working instead of staying home and spending their winnings? Why have the children of the Kennedy, Rockefeller, and Harriman families chosen to go into lives of public service instead of living off their trust funds? I suspect they need the psychological income of demonstrating their competence and giving something to the world. That is why so many men become depressed and develop health problems when they are laid off or retire. Studies have shown that men are more likely to be hospitalized for depression because of the loss of a job than because of the death of a family member. And that may be why so many noncareer women suffer from the "empty nest" syndrome when the last child leaves the house, and why so many widows are eager to remarry, not to have someone to take care of them but to have someone they can take care of. That is their "work," by which they assert their competence and make a difference to the world. Psychologist Pauline Bart writes of her experience trying to interview a middle-aged Jewish woman who had been hospitalized for depression. She could not take a case history because the woman kept on asking *her* questions: "Are you married?" "Why are you so thin?" "Do you cook for yourself?" "Why do you wear so much makeup?" The woman was depressed because she had no one to be a mother to. Like the depressed male patient down the hall, she felt "unemployed" and therefore worthless.

Work lets us feel creative. When the serpent was tempting Eve to eat the forbidden fruit, he offered her the prospect of becoming like God. God creates, as we find Him doing in the opening verses of the Bible. When we human beings create, when we make something which would not exist without us, we can feel a bit like God. It may be that when Adam and Eve forfeited their access to the Tree of Life by eating from the Tree of Knowledge, God set them down outside of Eden and told them to work and to bear children *as a cure for their mortality,* not as part of the punishment. Through children, we gain biological immortality and the perpetuation of our name and our values. Through our work, we leave evidence behind of who we were and what we were good at. Tracy Kidder, in his book about computers, *The Soul of a New Machine,* describes the feelings of engineers who had just finished designing and building a new computer. They speak of "self-fulfillment, a feeling of accomplishment, knowing that the thing you designed actually works the way you expected it would." One engineer even imagines that this must have been how God felt when He looked at the world He had made and pronounced it good. Work as punishment, as estrangement from a fulfilling life? It hardly sounds like it.

Several years ago, when my metamorphosis from congregational rabbi to bestselling author gave me a measure of freedom I had never had before, my wife and I set off on a six-week vacation trip to New Zealand, Australia, and the South Pacific. By the fifth week, I found myself getting edgy and restless. I couldn't understand why. We were doing enjoyable things in idyllic settings. Why had I stopped enjoying it as much as I had enjoyed the first month? Then I realized: I was suffering withdrawal symptoms from my work. For more than a month, I had not been doing the things by which I defined myself. No writing, no lecturing, no conducting services, no counseling troubled parishioners. It was as if, by not doing any of those things, I had stopped being me. It wasn't the money; it was the work as a way of testing and proclaiming who I was and what I could do. (Apparently I was able to do without it for a month before it got to me; some people have trouble doing that for a long weekend.)

I would even insist that when work is done in the right frame of mind, work can be holy. There is a linguistic connection between the words "work" and "worship." Work can be a way of serving God. Whatever we do for a living, we can learn to see it not only for the money we earn, but in terms of the blessings and benefits it brings other people. My colleague Rabbi Jeffrey Salkin has written a book, *Being God's Partner*, about a spiritual approach to our work. In it, he describes a man who works for a moving-van company and brings a religious approach to his work. The man explains that moving is stressful for most people. They are unsure about what awaits them in their new community. When he makes the experience of packing and shipping their belongings a pleasant, stress-free one by his attitude, when he speaks to them of the new opportunities which are theirs, he believes he is serving God by making those people less fearful.

Rabbi Salkin writes of a lingerie saleswoman who sanctifies her otherwise ordinary job by being especially sensitive and compassionate to the mastectomy patients who come to her store. When our son-in-law completed his orthodontic training at Boston University's dental school, he invited me to say a few words to his classmates at their graduation party. I told them, "When people ask you, 'What do you do?' don't tell them, 'I'm an orthodontist,' or 'I put braces on people's teeth.' Tell them, 'I help people have beautiful smiles and feel good about themselves.' It will not only be good for business; it will help you feel good about your work."

So much for Adam's "curse," the human impulse to express ourselves through our work. What about Eve's "curse," the human hunger for love? Again our misreading of the Garden of Eden story has left us with a lot of confused feelings about our sexuality. We misunderstand the story if we find in it the idea that sexuality is linked to sin, that lust is the result of Eve's disobedience and that the anguish of sexual longing is God's punishment for what our first ancestors did. Our religions may teach us to mistrust our bodies. Our early experiences with sex — the young girl who is molested by a relative, the dirty jokes and crude language in which we first learn to discuss sex, the painful fumbling rejections we all go through when we are young — may leave us with the impression that sex is sordid, dangerous, or exploitative.

But the real lesson of the Garden of Eden story is very different from all of those distorted lessons, different from Augustine's encounter with human willfulness or Milton's lament for the corruption of something perfect. The Bible's message about sexuality is this: the difference between human beings and animals is that, having the knowledge of Good and Evil, we introduce a moral dimension into our sexual behavior. For animals, there are right and wrong ways of mating, but only in a physical sense. "Right" means more likely to result in the birth of healthy offspring. For humans, right and wrong ways of meeting our sexual needs are so much more complicated. There are issues of lying and loyalty, of jealousy and possessiveness, of sensitivity and caring, that overwhelm the basic issue of reproduction.

Robert Wright, in his well-reasoned book *The Moral Animal*, would persuade us that a lot of what we think of as chosen sexual behavior based on our values is really a matter of our genetic inheritance. We resemble the animals more than we might like to think. Among humans and animals alike, males look for females who are likely to provide them with many healthy children (think of those Bible stories in which the worst thing that could happen to a woman would be barrenness), and females will only accept as a mate a male who seems willing and able to stay around and help raise and protect those children. Among humans and other species, it matters greatly to males that the children they are supporting are biologically theirs. These are not moral values, Wright insists. These are the blind strivings of our DNA to replicate itself and ensure its survival.

I suspect that there is a lot of truth to Wright's arguments. Every time I see a wealthy older man with an attractive young wife, often a second marriage (reminding me of the cynical aphorism "Many a man owes his success to his first wife, and owes his second wife to his success"), every time I read about a young child being abused by the mother's new boyfriend who is not the child's father, I see Wright's biological determinism at work.

But biology is not the whole story. Human beings are animals, but we are animals fashioned in the image of God. I have known husbands and wives who have continued to love each other, who have loved each other even more tenderly, after learning that one of them was infertile. I have known many, many cases of parents loving an adopted child, to whom they had no biological link, as an expression of their human impulse to raise a child, not their biological impulse to provide immortality to their genetic material. What makes us human, after all, is our ability to impose a layer of morality on the biological inheritance we share with other species. And we can thank Adam and Eve for that.

Eve's "curse" was not only that childbirth and parenting would be painful, but that sexual attraction would be painful as well. It is a scary thing to love someone, to let yourself *need* someone to feel fulfilled. You leave yourself so vulnerable to being hurt if that person leaves you, if he or she rejects you, or if he or she dies. As a result, many people are afraid to love, because it leaves them vulnerable. Barbra Streisand may sing, "People who need people are the luckiest people in the world," but a lot of her listeners seem to act on the assumption that people who *don't* need other people are the lucky ones. That way, no one can ever hurt you by leaving you.

Some years ago, a young couple came to see me in my study. They were to be married at my synagogue that summer, and they wanted to meet me and discuss the Jewish wedding ceremony with me. At one point, the young man said, "Rabbi Kushner, would you be willing to make one small change in the ceremony? Instead of pronouncing us husband and wife 'till death do us part,' could you pronounce us husband and wife for as long as our love lasts? We've talked about this, and we both agree that if we ever come to the point where we no longer love each other, it's not right for us to be stuck with each other."

I told him that I was sorry but I could

not make that change. I said to the couple, "I have some idea where you are coming from. Maybe you took the measure of your parents' marriage when you were growing up, saw the boredom, the resentment, maybe even saw them go through a bitter divorce. And you vowed that you would never end up like that. Maybe you had a good friend who trusted someone and was badly hurt by that person, or maybe you were hurt by someone you gave your heart to. And you resolved that you would never let anyone get close enough to you to hurt you like that again. But what I'm hearing is that both of you are afraid to give yourselves totally to this marriage for fear that it will hurt too much if it doesn't work out. So you're limiting your investment in it to minimize your possible losses. You're looking for intimacy without permanence, closeness without real commitment, and as long as you do that, you will never come to know what real intimacy and real commitment feel like."

Does it have to be so hard? Does the quest for love have to include so many broken hearts, so much coercion and rejection? Sometimes I think we would be better off going back to a world of arranged marriages, until I stop and think about whom my parents might have wanted to marry me off to and how often people who I thought were "absolutely right for each other" never struck a spark when I succeeded in introducing them to each other.

It may be that, in the search for love as in so many other areas of life, we do people no favor by screening out the pain and making life easier for them. Maybe we need to go through the experience of rejecting and being rejected to appreciate what a miracle it is to be accepted. Psychiatrist Willard Gaylin has written, "All of us must act selfishly to learn charity, must lie to learn honor, must betray and be betrayed to learn to value trust and commitment."

Because it hurts so much when love goes sour, because it hurts so much more when we lose a person who has become part of us, whether lost to death or rejection, than it does to lose someone we are merely fond of, some philosophers and some religious teachers teach us to protect ourselves against pain by not letting ourselves become too attached to anything impermanent. Love your job too much and you will be distraught if you lose it. Love your favorite dress too much and you will fall apart if the cleaners ruin it. Love your child too much and you give that child a formidable weapon with which to control you. Ration your love, limit your caring, they tell us, and you will never suffer the pain that God forecast for Eve and her daughters.

Why do we insist on loving, despite the risks? Dogs mate because they are driven wild by instinctive lust. Human beings search for love, not because we are blinded by lust and not because God has condemned us to anguish, but because there is a part of us that "remembers" the myth that once, long ago, each of us was not a separate individual but was part of something larger. We feel incomplete until we find that other person who restores our wholeness, who shows us how to escape the loneliness of being a self-sufficient individual by joining with someone else to "become one flesh." Painful? Yes, even at its most gratifying, love can be painful and leave us vulnerable to being hurt. Punishment? I would insist it is not.

It is harder to make a case for the third element of God's decree to Adam and Eve. Is there any sense in which we can call death good? Some religions try to ease the pain by denying the reality or the finality of death. We don't really die, they tell us. We just relocate to another world, where we are reunited with our loved ones who preceded us there. Death is a "graduation" from the frustrations and vulnerabilities of this world, a release from bodily lusts and limits. Some teachers promise us that we will live again after we die, as we have lived other lives before this one. Death is not forever. Christianity offers us the cross at the end of the biblical story as a parallel to the Tree of Life at the beginning, restoring to Adam's descendants what his misbehavior deprived us of. Jewish liturgy speaks of the Torah as a Tree of Life, planting the seeds of immortality within us. Survivors of near-death experiences are cited to reassure us that dying will not be painful. It will be a warm, comfortable experience. But I have lost too many people to death, and miss them too much, to be able to bring myself to say that death is in any way good or harmless. Death is terrible, disruptive, and final.

I once attended a conference of hospice workers, wonderful, dedicated people who sit by the bedsides of the terminally ill and make the process of dying less lonely and less frightening. One speaker warned her audience of the danger of using terms like "death management," saying, "We come to believe that we can 'manage' death, and in the process we forget what an awful, chaotic force death is. Death cannot be 'managed,' it can only be endured and survived."

But eating of the Tree of Knowledge did not condemn Adam and Eve to die. Animals die. It conferred on them the *knowledge* that they would one day die, and it is that awareness, more than the experience of death itself, that is the unique burden of a human being.

I will not make the claim that dying or having someone close to you die is a good thing, although I suspect that the alternative, living forever without ever dying, would be unbearable. In one chapter of Swift's *Gulliver's Travels*, Gulliver encounters a handful of people who are fated never to die, and they are the most pitiable of creatures. But is there a sense in which *knowing* that we are mortal, painful and terrifying as that knowledge may be, can make our lives richer and more truly human?

The first thing we have to do is free ourselves of the idea that death is a punishment. Humanity was not condemned to die because all people inevitably sin, and individuals (with the exception of criminals who are legally executed) do not die as a punishment for having sinned. Because we so desperately want our world to make sense in every detail, we are tempted to respond to another's death or misfortune by saying, "There must be a good reason why God did this to him." And we are tempted to respond to our own misfortunes and life-threatening illnesses by asking, "What did I do to deserve this?" For some reason, we feel better if we can identify something we did that was so terrible that it merited such punishment. That restores our faith that the world makes sense. But chances are that you have not done anything to deserve bad luck or bad health. The inescapable truth is that people get sick who do not deserve to be sick, and people die who do not deserve to die. You don't have to be a sinner to die; everyone does. In Dostoyevsky's novel *The Brothers Karamazov*, there is an incident in which a beloved old religious leader dies. The superstitious Russian peasants believe that, because he was a saint, his body will not deteriorate after death. When it begins to decay a day or two later, they are puzzled. Instead of concluding that death befalls good people and bad people alike, they begin to wonder if the old man was really that saintly after all.

I don't understand why so many people are reluctant to face the truth that sickness and death are not a punishment for wrongdoing. That perspective frees us to console the dying and their families without in any way feeling that we are giving aid and comfort to someone God wishes to punish. It frees us of the unrealistic notion that if we can be perfect enough, we will be immune to illness and death, because those things only happen to people who deserve them. And it keeps us from despair and disappointment with ourselves and from finding a connection between our inevitably being less than perfect and our discovering signs of age and decline in our bodies as we grow older.

A knowledge of our mortality makes us take life more seriously. Albert Schweitzer once wrote, "We must all become familiar with the thought of death if we want to grow into really good people. . . . Thinking about death produces love for life." Time is precious because we know we have a limited supply of it and there is no way we can buy more. Young people can be comfortable wasting time, wishing time would go by faster in their impatience for the next milestone in their lives, because they assume they have an endless supply of it. Young men make the best soldiers and the worst drivers because they cannot imagine themselves dying. But I have often been invited to speak to high school students after a classmate had died in an automobile accident (or in one case, after a drug overdose), and I have seen them work their way through the pain, the anger, and the bewilderment to confront the unwelcome message of their own vulnerability. Young people who have been through that will never take time or life for granted. They will use them differently, having seen how suddenly they can be lost.

The knowledge that our years are limited makes our choices matter. If we had all the time in the world, if we could indeed live forever, what we chose to do would not matter as much. What we didn't do today, what we got wrong today, we could get around to doing right somewhere down the line. In Homer's *Odyssey*, the sea goddess Calypso is envious of Odysseus and other humans precisely because they are mortal. Every choice is a courageous act of ruling out all the things that we will never do because there will not be time enough for all of them.

This knowledge of our mortality gives us the opportunity to declare that certain things — our families, our country, our faith — are supremely valuable to us because we are willing to risk losing our lives to defend them, and by implication other things — our jobs, our possessions — are less valuable because we are not prepared to die for them. Over the years, I have read a prayer at many memorial services that speaks of how we invest our lives with meaning by dedicating them to lofty and sacred goals. I believe that, but I also believe that it works the other way around as well. We hallow those causes and identify them as lofty and sacred by attaching the most valuable thing we own, our lives, to them. The years 1994–1995 marked the fiftieth anniversary of some of the climactic battles of World War II. I had many occasions over those months to talk to men who had fought in those battles when they were eighteen or twenty years old and remembered them a half century later. Some of them had been wounded, most of them had seen friends die, all of them had been scared, and all of them had left several prime years of their lives on the battlefields of Europe and the Pacific. But one after another, these seventy-year-old men brightened visibly and came alive as they spoke of those days. What they were remembering was not the mud and the danger. They were remembering the experience of caring enough about something to put their lives on the line for what they cherished.

Coming to terms with the fact that we

will one day die should teach us compassion for the elderly, the crippled, the infirm. Because we are a death-fearing, death-denying society, we are made uncomfortable by anyone who reminds us of our ultimate fate, the inescapable reality of death. Philanthropist George Soros, speaking at Columbia University's inauguration of a project to help Americans understand the phenomena of death and grief, said, "In America, the land of the perpetually young, growing old is an embarrassment and dying is seen as a failure." As long as we cherish the fantasy that, by exercising and lowering our cholesterol, we can cheat death and live forever, we will be embarrassed by the elderly, the sick, and the dying. They will challenge our illusions of immortality. So we will segregate the aged in retirement villages and nursing homes, where we will visit them as infrequently as we can. We will avoid visiting the seriously ill in their hospital rooms. Only when we give up the impossible and unworthy dream of immortality (Chesterton once wrote, "There are people who pray for eternal life and don't know what to do with themselves on a rainy Sunday"), only when we learn to see the fate of the aging and the dying as *our* fate as well as theirs, will we be able to share their last adventure with them and learn from them how to live out *our* days.

The fifth of the Ten Commandments bids us honor our parents "that your days may be long upon the earth." I am not sure that people who honor their parents live longer than people who don't. Maybe what the Bible is suggesting is that, if we fashion a society in which the elderly are cherished and taken seriously, we will be able to look forward to growing old ourselves instead of dreading it. We will not have to lie about our ages, dye our hair, visit the plastic surgeon, because growing old is an embarrassment. We will not shun the elderly for fear of becoming like them. We will revere them for the living lesson they represent.

How would you define a "good death"? In the Middle Ages, a good death was a death that did not come until you had made your peace with God and prepared your soul for the Last Judgment. That is why Hamlet refuses to kill his treacherous uncle at prayer; the man did not deserve that clean a death. Most people today would define a good death as one that took them unaware, without forcing them to confront the prospect of dying, "to go to sleep one night and not wake up." (Or they might fall back on the old line that a good death would be living to age ninety and being shot by a jealous husband.)

Let me suggest my own definition: a good death would be one that does not contradict what your life has been about. It permits us to be the same person dying as we were when we were alive. I think of three people I admired greatly who were not that fortunate, the writer Primo Levi, the psychologist Lawrence Kohlberg, and the former Episcopal bishop of New England, David Johnson. Levi was a survivor of Auschwitz. He went on to write several deeply moving books about his experiences there. Every page he wrote was a testament to the human being's ability to survive the most demonic circumstances. Kohlberg, a professor at Harvard, did groundbreaking research on the development of a sense of morality in children and adults. He set forth the model of the man or woman who courageously acts on principle, no matter how unpopular, as the highest level of maturity. Johnson was a beloved religious leader who vigorously defended the rights of the marginal in the religious community. All three ended up taking their own lives, Levi in apparent despair over a family situation, Kohlberg because of the physical pain of an incurable disease, and Johnson because of the pending revelation of some improper behavior in his ecclesiastical office. I do not pass judgment on them; I pray I never find myself in the situations they were in at the end of their lives. But for me, the tragedy of their deaths is not that their lives were cut short, but that the manner of their dying was so at odds with the message of their lives and work, a message of courage, hope, and forgiveness. I fear that their personal despair will make it harder for people to accept the truths of their teaching, and I find that terribly sad.

Many years ago, an older and wiser colleague taught me the secret of composing a eulogy when I officiate at a funeral. He said, "Every human being's life is a story, a unique story that nobody ever lived before and no one will ever live again. Your task is to identify that unique story and put it into words." When we learn to think of life as a story, then we can come to think of death not as punishment but as punctuation. What we want to know about a book or movie is not how long it is, but how good it is, and we can learn to think of life in the same way. If life is a story, then we understand it better as we get closer to the end. Only then can we understand the real significance of something that happened back in chapter three or four. If life is a story, we can wish it would go on forever, but we understand that even the best of stories has to end. It would be a strange story if it did go on forever. So instead of grieving that it had to end, we can feel blessed that we were lucky enough to have been part of it.

There is a brief passage in the Bible, in chapter 48 of the Book of Genesis, that never fails to move me. The patriarch Jacob is on his deathbed and is looking back over his long and eventful life. In an age when most people never traveled outside the village of their birth, he has lived in three countries. He has made and lost fortunes. But of all that has happened to him, the one thing he remembers is that his beloved wife Rachel died when they were young. I read the account of his remembering the loss, and in my own mind I add the words that I suspect Jacob was thinking but not saying aloud: "Rachel died, and somehow I survived her death, and every day since then I have thought about her, and that act of remembering has kept her in my life."

Only human beings can do that. Only human beings can defeat death by summoning up the memory of someone they loved and lost, and feeling that person close to them as they do so.

When we are young, we turn to religion to help us find our way in the world, to make us prosperous, to make our dreams come true. When we reach middle age, we turn to religion to give us peace of mind and peace of soul. But when we grow old, we turn to religion to help us defeat death, our own and that of the people we love. We pray that the biopsy result will be favorable, that the surgery will succeed, that the illness will pass. And when we reluctantly conclude that God cannot keep us alive indefinitely no matter how good or pious we are, we ask Him to teach us to conquer death in another way, by giving us the blessing of memory.

Memory can be painful, as everything that makes a human being more than an animal can be painful. Good memories deepen the poignancy of what we have lost. Bad memories keep the resentment alive when the occasion is long past. But memory is what ultimately gives us power over death, by keeping the person alive in our hearts. Memory is what gives us power over time, by keeping the past present so that it cannot fade and rob us of what we once held precious. And as far as we know, only human beings have that. In a sense, our time on earth is limited, but in another sense it is not. We not only have today; we have all the yesterdays we are capable of remembering and all the tomorrows we can envision.

Chapter 8

HOW GOOD DO WE HAVE TO BE?

We start out, when we are young, trying so hard to be perfect because we want to please our parents and because we are terribly afraid of losing their love by doing something wrong. Occasionally parents, distracted and inexperienced, do something to reinforce that fear. But if we are lucky, most of the time they forgive us and reassure us that their love is constant.

We fall in love and imagine the person we love to be perfect, because it would reflect so well on us if he or she were. And then, when we inevitably find faults in our mate and he or she finds faults in us, we need to summon up the power of forgiveness to sustain the marriage, choosing happiness over righteousness.

We may have been taught that God sees our every deed and reads our every secret thought, and we were sure that He was disappointed in us. We may have been haunted by the story of Adam and Eve, and thought to ourselves, "If God did that to people who committed one small sin, what punishments does He have in store for me for all the things I've done wrong?" But we can come to see God as a God of forgiveness who understands our human nature as a blend of the animal and the divine. Resembling God in our knowledge of good and evil, we try to rise, but our animal nature keeps pulling us down, keeps us earthbound. We aspire and stumble, and God loves us in our aspiring and in our stumbling.

The Bible's last word on the Garden of Eden tells us that God stationed an angel with a flaming sword at the entrance to the garden (Genesis 3:24) so that Adam and Eve could never return and eat of the Tree of Life. But from time to time, their descendants do try to return to Eden.

Sometimes people try to reclaim Eden by creating a Utopia, a perfect society where there will be no poverty, no crime, no envy. Communities like that sprang up in the American Midwest in the nineteenth century. Such a vision inspired some leaders of the French and Russian revolutions. Martin Buber hailed the Israeli kibbutz, the collective farm on which there is no private property, as an effort to remove selfishness from economic effort. But inevitably such societies discover that human beings are not meant to create perfection. Human frailties inevitably appear and spoil the utopian effort. (I am reminded of the habit of Inuit artisans in Alaska deliberately to introduce a flaw into their weaving and sculpting so as not to offend God by trying to fashion something perfect.)

On other occasions, people strive to re-create the Garden of Eden by temporarily going back to a time before we knew the difference between Good and Evil, between Right and Wrong, a time when we could behave like children, like animals, doing what we felt like doing and not being held responsible for our actions because we could not be expected to know that they were wrong. The pre-Lenten carnivals in Brazil and other places, when ordinary rules of dress and behavior are temporarily suspended, or the nude, drunken revels of young people at Woodstock in the 1960's are examples of wanting to go back to Eden, to a world where Adam and Eve could be naked without shame and behave without rules of what is "permitted" and what is "forbidden." The traditional office Christmas party, the celebrations when the home team wins a championship, and other occasions when people are given tacit permission to get drunk and act irresponsibly are further examples. Human beings want to be held accountable as moral beings. We want to be considered responsible for our actions, rather than being treated like children or mentally defective people who don't understand what they are doing. But from time to time, the garments of morality chafe and bind and we want to throw them off. (Omar Khayyám wrote, "Come, fill the Cup, and in the fire of Spring / The Winter garment of Repentance fling.") We resent Adam and Eve for ever having eaten the forbidden fruit and bequeathing a knowledge of Right and Wrong to us.

But there is no going back to Eden, as the Bible warns us. We *are* human beings, blessed and burdened with a conscience, and we cannot pretend to be children, no matter how much fun that might be.

There is a key passage in Steinbeck's *East of Eden* (in my edition, it comes on the exact middle page of the book and reoccurs on the very last page) in which Mr. Lee, the Chinese cook who is the book's moral anchor, tells a fascinating story about joining four elderly Chinese gentlemen in two years of studying Hebrew so that they could properly understand one verse in the Bible. It was important for them to know the precise meaning of what God said to Cain. Did God say, "Sin crouches at the door but *thou shalt* rule over it," as in the King James translation? Did God say, "*Do thou* rule over it," as the American Standard Bible has it? After two years, they decided that both translations were wrong. The true meaning of God's word *timshol* was "*Thou mayest* rule over it." Mr. Lee goes on, "Don't you see? The American Standard *orders* men to triumph over sin. The King James makes a *promise* in 'thou shalt.' But the Hebrew 'thou mayest' gives us a *choice*. It might be the most important word in the Bible!"

It is a wonderful story — four elderly Chinese men studying Hebrew, writing Hebrew characters in Chinese ink with a brush — and it is crucial to Steinbeck's intention in writing *East of Eden*. But I have been studying biblical Hebrew for fifty years, I earned my doctorate in biblical Hebrew, and I still can't say for certain what *timshol* and many other key biblical words mean. No one can. We can only make the best guess we can, colored inevitably by our theological biases. Many biblical verses are like inkblot tests, revealing more about us than about the text in question.

But more importantly, *timshol* is the wrong word if we want to know what God expects of us (though it is the right word for Steinbeck's narrative purposes). My candidate for the most important single word in the Bible occurs in Genesis 17:1, when God says to Abraham, "Walk before Me and be *tamim.*" What does that word mean? The King James Bible translates it as "perfect"; the Revised Standard Version takes it to mean "blameless." If they are correct, then God would indeed expect us to be perfect, always doing the right thing and never sinning. (The same word, *tamim,* is used elsewhere in the Bible to describe an animal fit to be offered on God's altar because it is without blemish.)

But more recent translations, for a combination of linguistic and theological reasons, have backed away from the notion of God demanding that Abraham (and we) be perfect and without flaw. The animals brought to God's altar might have to be perfect and unblemished, but the human beings bringing them cannot be expected to be. Contemporary scholars take the word *tamim* to mean something like "wholehearted." My own study of the verse leads me to conclude that what God wants from Abraham, and by implication from us, is not perfection but integrity. God wants Abraham to strive to be true to the core of who he is, even if he strays from that core occasionally. As the folk saying puts it, "I'm not much, Lord, but I'm all I've got." Or as Mother Teresa once told an interviewer, "We are not here to be successful; we are here to be faithful," which I would take to mean faithful to our essential selves as well as to God.

God knows us all too well to demand perfection of us. Why would God set us up for failure, establishing a standard that none of us could meet? One of the strangest passages in all of Scripture occurs in the nineteenth chapter of the Book of Numbers. If a person feels contaminated by something he has done wrong and does not feel worthy of coming into God's presence, that person can cleanse and purify himself by undergoing the ritual of the Red Heifer. A cow with entirely red skin, without a single discolored hair, is sacrificed, and its ashes made into a paste that is applied to the person to purify him. Even in the biblical context of animal offerings, the ritual of the Red Heifer is very strange. I never understood it until a colleague offered this theory: the Red Heifer, the animal without a single blemish or discoloration, represents perfection. It is slaughtered to make the point that perfection has no place in this world. Perfect creatures belong in heaven, not on earth. This world is for those of us who are struggling with our imperfections.

Some years ago, my wife and I were traveling in Mexico. We visited the ruins of once-great Aztec cities, and our guide tried to explain to us the significance of the Ball Court, a prominent feature of each of the sites. (As he did, I imagined archaeologists of the future trying to explain to their contemporaries the significance of the baseball and football stadiums we have built.) The ball game was more than an athletic event in Aztec culture. It was a competition with religious-ritual meaning. According to some records, at the end of the game, the losing team would be sacrificed to the gods (as I can imagine many fans today wanting to do when their team loses). But according to other records, it was the *winning* team that was sacrificed! And if that was the case, I found myself wondering if there is something in the human soul that wants to destroy winners as our way of saying, as the Israelites said about the Red Heifer, that perfection belongs only in heaven; this world is for flawed, imperfect people like us.

The Israeli writer S. Y. Agnon, who won the Nobel Prize for Literature in 1966, first gained fame for his short novel *The Crooked Shall Be Made Straight*, published in Hebrew in 1912 and unfortunately never translated into English. *The Crooked Shall Be Made Straight* is the story of a simple, decent man named Menashe. He cannot make a living in his grocery store because he is too kind to ask for money from people who cannot pay, and too decent to match the tactics of his ruthless competitors. He has to close his store and has no alternative but to go from town to town begging. The rabbi of his village gives him a letter testifying to the fact that he is a good and honest man who deserves to be helped.

Menashe spends a year on the road collecting charity. With the help of the rabbi's letter, he collects enough money to be able to go back and start a new business. On his last night before he heads for home, he lodges at an inn where he meets a man who is in every way his opposite, a thief, a liar, and a conniver. The thief sees Menashe's letter and says, "If I had a letter like that, I could do very well." He offers Menashe a substantial sum of money to sell him the letter, which after all he no longer needs. Menashe is tempted by the money and sells the letter. With more money than he has ever had before, Menashe goes to town to celebrate his good fortune. There he gets drunk and is robbed of everything he has, even his prayer shawl. Lacking even the money to travel home, he has to begin asking for charity all over again.

Meanwhile the thief is set upon by highwaymen and killed, his body mutilated beyond recognition. When the body is found, with Menashe's letter in a pocket, word is sent to Menashe's village that he has died. The rabbi declares that although the evidence of his death is circumstantial, it would be cruel to keep his wife in suspense indefinitely, and declares her a widow, free to remarry. Several months later, she remarries, and a year later gives birth to a son.

Meanwhile the real Menashe has painfully worked his way home. He arrives in town on the day his wife and her new husband are celebrating the ritual circumcision of their child. He now faces a terrible dilemma. If he declares himself alive, his wife will be found to be an adulteress, however inadvertent, and her child branded illegitimate, an outcast in the Jewish community. He cannot do that to someone he loves. Instead, he chooses to live outside of town, in the cemetery. He tells his sad story to the custodian of the cemetery, who takes pity on him, keeps his secret, and brings him food. Shortly after that, Menashe dies, and the custodian buries him by the memorial stone his wife had set up for him when she thought him dead two years earlier.

What is that story trying to tell us? I once had the opportunity to meet Agnon when I was studying in Israel. A group of us were invited to his home for tea and conversation. One of our number asked him what he was trying to say in *The Crooked Shall Be Made Straight*. Was it a criticism of religion? Of God's justice? Agnon smiled and said, "I only write stories. I leave it to my critics to understand them." I think one of Agnon's central messages is that when you compromise your integrity, you lose everything. Menashe was not a perfect person, but he was a good one. However, when he sold the letter, he was acting out of character. For the first time in his life, he was doing something deceitful for a quick, dishonest profit. When he sold the letter, he literally gave away his good name. And by giving away his good name, it was as if the real Menashe ceased to exist. Only when he performed an act of immense self-sacrifice did he reestablish himself as a man of decency and integrity (ironically, by permitting an illegal relationship to continue), and as a result, he got his name back. He found his final resting place beneath a gravestone with his name on it.

When we do something wrong, because

we are human and our choices are so complicated and temptations so strong, we don't lose our humanity. But we lose our integrity, our sense of wholeness, of being the same person all the time. We create a situation where a part of us, our good self, is at war with another part of us, our weak and selfish side. We lose the focus, the singleness of purpose, that enables us to do the things that matter to us. That is when we need the religious gift of forgiveness and atonement (making our split selves *at one*). But should we ever conclude that there is no point in trying to be good because we can never be good enough, that is when we lose everything. Being human can never mean being perfect, but it should always mean struggling to be as good as we can and never letting our failures be a reason for giving up the struggle.

How good can we expect a person to be? How much goodness can we expect of ourselves? I had lunch one day with a young man who was thinking of entering the Christian ministry. His father was a friend of mine and thought that we would enjoy meeting each other. Our talk focused on our theological differences, not in any effort to convert or disprove each other but out of a desire to understand the other's perspective presented at its best and clearest. Before long, we identified the point at which our views, which largely overlapped, parted company. The cornerstone of his religious worldview was his notion of "the essential depravity of Man." People might do some good things from time to time, but were essentially willful and selfish. Even the good things they did might be selfishly motivated. The basis of my religious outlook, by contrast, was the essential decency of Man. People, in a moment of fear or weakness, might do shameful things, but except for the occasional psychopath, they were troubled by their wrongdoing and motivated to atone for it. People were not good, I suggested, but they were capable of goodness.

He reminded me of the Holocaust (as if I needed to be reminded), and I reminded him of the hundreds of Christians who risked their lives to help Jews. He referred to the persistent rates of violent crime, and I told him of the Duke University study indicating that honest, cheerful, generous people tended to be healthier than suspicious, selfish, hostile ones. Since we each had our newspaper headlines and personal anecdotes to "prove" our position, we left the issue unresolved and concentrated on lunch.

In the mid-nineteenth century, some religious conservatives attacked Charles Darwin for his theory of evolution, which suggested that humankind had evolved from lower species rather than being a special creation of God as described in Genesis. But others fastened on Darwin's theory of "the survival of the fittest" as proof of the "essential depravity of Man." Because of limited resources (not enough food, land, or sexual partners for everyone), human beings would inevitably see other human beings as competitors and enemies, and invest their energies in struggling against them. Human life would be marked by hatred, jealousy, and war, as it has been since the day Adam and Eve left Paradise and Cain killed Abel.

In 1991, Stephen Jay Gould, who teaches science at Harvard and is a gifted essayist, published a collection of his writings, *Bully for Brontosaurus*, which introduced me to the thought of Petr Kropotkin, a Russian naturalist and a critic of Darwin. Kropotkin suggested that seeing life as a constant struggle over limited food and space might have come naturally to Darwin, who lived in England, a crowded country with few natural resources. But Kropotkin lived in Russia, a large, underpopulated country, and the lesson he learned from nature was not the lesson of men competing against each other for limited rewards, but of people *cooperating* with each other in a struggle against a harsh environment. Yes, only the fittest survive, but the "fittest" are the ones best able to cooperate with their neighbors, to engage in mutual protection and helpfulness, not the strong ones who can overpower the weak and leave themselves with few friends and allies to help them through the winter. Gould describes Kropotkin as becoming "more and more convinced that the cooperative style, leading to mutual aid, not only predominated in general but also characterized the most advanced creatures in any group, ants among insects, mammals among vertebrates. Mutual aid therefore becomes a more important principle than competition."

The love of a parent for a child, the willingness to share food and even risk her life for her child, is natural. It guarantees the future; it perpetuates the species. But altruism, the willingness to give of yourself to help a stranger, is not natural. Yet people do it. People give money to beggars and send charity to overseas relief agencies. People jump into lakes and run into burning buildings to save the lives of strangers. People stay up all night answering a suicide hot line. That is not natural, but it *is* human nature, the unique ability of human beings to feel the pain of a stranger and want to do something to alleviate it. I believe that my point of view of what it means to be human explains acts of cruelty better than the pessimist's view of "the essential depravity of Man" explains acts of compassion. How good can we expect a person to be? As good as he or she is capable of being, and much of the time that turns out to be very good indeed.

As I began this book with an observation about Yom Kippur, the Jewish Day of Atonement, let me conclude with another Yom Kippur episode. The most personal sermon I ever gave in thirty years as a rabbi was on Yom Kippur 1978. One year earlier, as Jews all over the world prayed to be inscribed in the Book of Life, our son, Aaron, was terminally ill. He died a few weeks later. I knew that my sermon on the first Yom Kippur after his death would have to be a major statement about what his death had meant to me and to my faith, and how I could go on believing in a world where young children died.

I took my text that morning not from the Bible but from a little book called *The Miss-*

ing Piece, by Shel Silverstein, which I can only describe as a fairy tale for adults. This is the story of *The Missing Piece*: Once there was a circle that was missing a piece. A large triangular wedge had been cut out of it. The circle wanted to be whole, with nothing missing, so it went around looking for its missing piece. But because it was incomplete, it could only roll very slowly as it rolled through the world. And as it rolled slowly, it admired the flowers along the way. It chatted with butterflies. It enjoyed the sunshine.

It found lots of pieces, but none of them fit. Some were too big and some were too small. Some were too square and some too pointy. So it left them all by the side of the road and kept on searching.

Then one day it found a piece that fit perfectly. It was so happy. Now it could be whole, with nothing missing. It incorporated the missing piece into itself and began to roll. Now that it was a perfect circle, it could roll very fast, too fast to notice the flowers, too fast to talk to the butterflies. When it realized how different the world seemed when it rolled through it so quickly, it stopped, left its missing piece by the side of the road, and rolled slowly away, looking for its missing piece.

I suggested in my sermon that the lesson of the story was that, in some strange sense, we are more whole when we are incomplete, when we are missing something. The man who has everything is in some ways a poor man. He will never know what it feels like to yearn, to hope, to nourish his soul with the dream of something better. He will never know the experience of having someone who loves him give him something he has always wanted and never had.

There is a wholeness about the person who can give himself away, who can give his time, his money, his strength, to others and not feel diminished when he does so. There is a wholeness about the person who has come to terms with his limitations, who knows who he is and what he can and cannot do, the person who has been brave enough to let go of his unrealistic dreams and not feel like a failure for doing so. There is a wholeness about the man or woman who has learned that he or she is strong enough to go through a tragedy and survive, the person who can lose someone through death, through divorce, through estrangement, and still feel like a complete person and not just part of a broken couple. At that point, nothing can scare you. You have been through the worst and come through it whole. When we have lost part of ourselves and can continue rolling through life and appreciating it, we will have achieved a wholeness that others can only aspire to.

That, I believe, was what God asked of Abraham. Not "Be perfect," not "Don't ever make a mistake," but "Be whole." To be whole before God means to stand before Him with all of our faults as well as all of our virtues, and to hear the message of our acceptability. To be whole means to rise beyond the need to pretend that we are perfect, to rise above the fear that we will be rejected for not being perfect. And it means having the integrity not to let the inevitable moments of weakness and selfishness become permanent parts of our character. Know what is good and what is evil, and when you do wrong, realize that that was not the essential you. It was because the challenge of being human is so great that no one gets it right every time. God asks no more of us than that.

The philosopher Immanuel Kant once wrote, "Out of timber as crooked as that which man is made of, nothing perfectly straight can be carved." He is probably right, but the lesson to be learned from that insight is not to give up on humanity, but to give up on the search for perfection.

Maybe human beings can't fashion anything perfectly straight. But maybe what we *are* able to fashion, with its curves and knotholes, will be more interesting, more satisfying.

Life is not a trap set for us by God, so that He can condemn us for failing. Life is not a spelling bee, where no matter how many words you have gotten right, if you make one mistake you are disqualified. Life is more like a baseball season, where even the best team loses one-third of its games and even the worst team has its days of brilliance. Our goal is not to go all year without ever losing a game. Our goal is to win more than we lose, and if we can do that consistently enough, then when the end comes, we will have won it all.

In the beginning, in the infancy of the human race as in the infancy of an individual human being, life was simple. Then we ate of the fruit of that tree and we gained the knowledge that some things are good and others are bad. We learned how painfully complex life could be.

But at the end, if we are brave enough to love, if we are strong enough to forgive, if we are generous enough to rejoice in another's happiness, and if we are wise enough to know that there is enough love to go around for us all, then we can achieve a fulfillment that no other living creature will ever know. We can reenter Paradise.